START Somewhere

Morgan Campbell

START Somewhere

Moving on to My Future by Forgetting My Past

Start Somewhere by Morgan Campbell

ISBN: 978-1-59755-793-1

Published by: ADVANTAGE BOOKS™
Orlando, FL
www.advbookstore.com

Library of Congress Catalog Number: 2024942219

Name:	Campbell, Morgan
Title:	Start Somewhere
	Morgan Campbell, Author
	Advantage Books, 2024
Identifiers:	ISBN Paperback: 9781597557931
Subjects:	Christian Life – Inspirational
	Biography / Autobiography
	Christian Life – Personal Growth

First Printing: August 2024
24 25 26 27 28 29 10 9 8 7 6 5 4 3 2 1

PROLOGUE

BEGINNINGS

Do I belong here…am I in the right place? I don't really know what's going on or how I should feel…I'm different from others…DUH! I don't fit in with certain "cliques," and I feel like nobody else thinks or acts like I do, but do they actually? I tend to think a lot about things and why they happen. Why is my family the way it is, is it all genetics, is it okay all this is happening, is it normal…is it my fault? I wonder what God has planned for me, will I really make a difference, or am I just here to be here? It sticks with me, why can't I just be "normal". Words spoken by most Americans…Is it normal for a ten-year-old to think about all this?

My life isn't like others, obviously. Most people have kids because they want to have kids, I feel like my dad just went with it because my mom wanted kids. He told her he never wanted kids, and she told me eventually as I got older, guess how that made me feel…it's fine. I totally suspected it from how he treats us. I guess I shouldn't feel this way; some other families are like this too, right?

I need to stop thinking about other people and think about myself. I tend to think of others too much and not focus on myself. I wonder what people think of me, because I'm awkward and feel ugly most of the time. I think others think so…people call me pretty, but I honestly question it sometimes? Anyway, parents have to say that, they're not gonna say you're ugly, right? I compare and think too much…Will I ever change?

Let me tell you about myself if you care to listen. I grew up near Chicago. I have an older brother. I like to think I'm funny, I am shy and awkward, and that makes me "Shawkward"! Need I say more? Little did I know what I was waiting for as I grew up. I had an okay childhood, I would say. I loved playing with my brother, cousin and her neighbors. We loved playing at the street fairs, kickball, chasing the ball up and down the hill. We'd yelling "car," moving to the side and pausing the game, so we don't get run over, playing video games together, playing tag, and not having a worry on life. I was too young to know what was really going on. I'm at home in my room, hearing my dad scream and hit my mom. What would you do? There wasn't really anything I could do, what does a seven-year-old do in that situation? Sometimes I would yell back at him or cry so he would hear it, but it didn't help much, he'd just ignore me or call me names, why would God let this happen?

I would yell a demonic scream at the top of my lungs for him to stop, and ask why he does this. He of course had no logical answer why he hits and screams at my mom, he would just yell and swear back at me to shut up and that I don't understand. Yeah, you're right, I don't understand why you're doing this, but I still love you anyway I guess.

He wasn't all bad, I guess, I call it now a love-hate relationship. I hate him sometimes, and then I love him other times…or I want to hate him but love him, anyway; I just don't show it at that time.

The good times I remember playing catch with him and laughing at his jokes, but I mainly tend to only focus on the not so good times, like him yelling and hitting my mom.

One of my many problems is I keep letting people in when they should stay out. I guess I'm just too nice of a person and can't shut people out. I'm the type of person who gives people second chances…or three or twenty. Anyway, you may never know someone's story or what they're going through, people may act like they're fine when they're really not…like my dad.

I tried to just brush the bad moments off, but they seemed to follow. I know now why I used to be so scared of storms, I was living in one. I can't comprehend how a person, who says they love us, can act like this. This is not love…or is it?

Nobody at school seemed to know or even care; I felt like I couldn't talk to anyone about it, I felt like they wouldn't understand, how does a fifth grader even ask for help? He just hits my mom and yells a lot, he's not hitting me so what's the problem? Do people actually care about this? Should people care? My mom would get big black bruises from him and lie about how she got them, saying she fell, or something like that. I figured no one needed or should know about this (also things would be "normal" the next day).

High School is when I really got help from the school counselor, but I waited until mid-freshman year, until something really bad happened, and he actually did hit me for the first time. It felt good to talk to someone, but I knew it would never erase what happened; people tell me to just not think about the bad times, but that's easier said than done.

Is this all worth it, do people really care about me? I feel like people just do things to be nice, even if they don't want to. I've witnessed people talking to other people, complaining to their friends about how annoying their other friends are. It makes me wonder if people do that to me. That's mainly the reason I don't talk much, because I don't want others to talk about me like that. I don't really know how people like me. Maybe it's just because I listen and smile when they talk? I don't really know…maybe it's all a fake? All I see is my past and how I'm not like others, but I guess that's what makes me special.

When I'm with friends back home I think about what I'm doing at college, what I'm missing out at home, how much I miss it. When we go out to lunch, have bonfires, laugh, we have a great time. I think about if college is worth all this money, if I'm really doing the money's worth, I mean I try to make it all worth it. If I leave college what am I, will people be sad or even notice I'm gone?

I just really want to know the future, just to know if I'm successful or not, doesn't everybody? I used to not worry about the future. However, you've kind of have to pick a major, think about what job you'll have for the rest of your life, does it pay well, can you see yourself doing it for about twenty years. Sounds like a lot of pressure for an 18-year old. I guess what people mean is don't WORRY about the future, you can think about it but you shouldn't worry about it. I think about the future a lot, but will eventually say everything is in God's hands, and that calms me a little…ish.

I was in math class my freshman year of high school; the teacher handed out a little assignment, asking us students what we did about our grades. When she collected the papers from the class of 30 students, she chose my anonymous answer to read aloud. "I don't worry about it," she didn't like that answer, but it was how I met my first friend…and when my worrying about the future began.

People judge me without even knowing me, they may think I have everything put together; or I'm so screwed up it's sad to even know me. I wish to show people who I really am, why I am who I am, and what I strive to be. I may be "Shawkward", but I'm much more than that…I think so at least; I just need confidence.

1

BREAKING

I don't really know how to explain myself; I think too much, stress too much, jealous, and think I am really different from others, is that a good enough explanation? I try not to be like this. It's like I think of all these things, have fun in my mind, but then don't say what's on my mind. Because I feel like people will shoot me down, or not understand what's up there, hell, I don't even know most of the time.

My body physically hurts, and my mind is exhausted from thinking too much. I can't concentrate in class, I'm tired, depressed, don't have many friends…hearing people laugh makes me annoyed sometimes, because I envy that feeling.

****

What do you do when you are depressed or don't know who you are? Some people cut themselves, listen to music, watch TV, get laid, cry, or do nothing. I usually listen to music, complain to friends, or cry. I have been depressed since 7th grade. Not majorly depressed…maybe…I didn't take my problem as seriously as I should have (also probably didn't know what depression was). I knew I wasn't as "bad" as others, like cutting myself everyday or coming to school with bruises. I kept my problems bottled up inside and cried about it later, which was not the best strategy. People probably didn't know I was depressed, because I hid it so well and rarely talked to people.

Who wants to hear about depression? When someone's having a good day and you go; "I'm depressed, can we talk?" First of all, that's a horrible conversation starter, and I feel bad dragging others into my life, even when they listen, do they want to? I don't want to be a downer, so I just hide my feelings and cry later.

Yes, I say I was and still am depressed because: I cut now and then knowing it's bad and I shouldn't. I over-think just about everything and it gets me upset. My life hasn't exactly been a 'joyride', if you know what I mean? But whose life has?

I feel like most people are depressed and say things like I want to die...so what's the big deal? The big deal is I see depressing jokes posted on social media everywhere. Most of them I think are quite funny, but in like a sad funny way. Like how I feel; that is why I find it normal people 'hate their lives' and are depressed, because it's so common it's even on social media.

Society makes this not a big deal, because almost everyone feels this way, but what can we do to stop it? Well, the only thing we really can do is not listen to society, which most people do, or just ignore the depressing posts. We like to normalize things and depression and sadness is normal, so why not crack a few jokes about it, let's make depression a little fun (ny).

The internet is a hoot: Act like this, be married and have a house and kids by this age, being gay is awesome, go vegan, go off the grid, and eat dirt. Okay maybe not the last one…the point is the internet has all these "rules," and for what, to be happy? Maybe…maybe eating dirt is the way to go? Who knows? It's different for everyone; society can help the forgotten (I'm still waiting).

I just really don't like most things society has become, like making jokes about depression and suicide. I feel comfortable seeing those jokes about 'life failing' things. It makes me feel like I'm not the only one that's failing…but on the other hand, they make me feel bad because I feel that way. I don't know…I don't know, I don't know, I don't Knooow! Whatever, it's fine, I'm fine. At least my friends like the posts when I share them. Then there's my family, asking if I'm okay, or threatening they're going to un-friend me because I share these things like 'sticking a fork in an outlet and calling it a day.

I feel my depression really took a turn for the worse when I was in college. I missed back home, my roommates weren't the best, I had no friends, and it was hard, go figure. I cried almost every night. I'd listening to music, miss my mom, contemplating life, lie in bed, and put on a smile around others. I'd wonder if I could really be successful, or if I'm just thinking about a fantasy life. I had no motivation to do anything, but I did anyway. That feeling sucks, it's like you're being forced to play a role you hate.

It was the second week of my freshman year at college. Still sad and depressed, I went to my theology class, not knowing my professor would actually relate to ME. I sat down with a sad look on my face, well, more like a mix between a confused, sad, and intrigued look on my face, if that makes sense...I'm bad at explaining things. I forgot what the lesson was about, but I will always remember what he said that day. He told a story about when he was a freshman in college and knows how we may feel: scared, alone, nervous, like we don't belong. And that's exactly what I felt; he ended by saying if we feel that way to come talk to him.

I was trying not to cry. Of course, being the emotional person I am, my eyes filled with tears. My eyes turned a light red. That feeling was building up. The feeling when you try not to cry as the pressure building up in your nose and your face feeling hot and red. I was casually covering my face with my hair so no one would see me. I softly played with my hair, placing it closer to my face so I couldn't see anyone. Therefore, they couldn't see me. He was such a great person I could connect to; I really wanted to talk with him.

****

I remembered him the first weekend of school; all the freshmen were in the auditorium listening to other people's experiences at this college and what to expect the first year. I will always remember what my Theology 105 professor said, "I like when students come to me with their problems"

That's when I woke up.

I paid my fullest attention to him when he said that, staring intently at him. He says he likes working through their problems with them. My heart kind of melting when he said that, because I feel like there aren't many people like him in this world, or at least anyone who admits to that. I tried not to cry, because my roommate was next to me, and I didn't want her to think I'm some weird emotional person. I thought maybe he could help me; I loved him and what he said, it was fate he was my professor.

Walking in on the first day of theology, I never would've guessed he'd actually be my professor, I was kind of happy when I saw he was. I was sitting there with my head kind of down, with a confused/ sad/ intrigued look on my face. He told his college story to us, and I sat there "not crying." He ended his story and class was over, I couldn't get out of there fast enough.

I came to him the next day after my class. I stood probably about five minutes outside the chapel doors, mustering the courage to walk in or not, and if this is worth talking with him about. I walked shyly through the chapel and up to his door; I stood in a knocking position for about a minute. When I was about to actually knock, he called my name from down the hallway. He knows my name, oh gosh, is it too late to just run away? No, that's not what people in college do. I walked in his office with him, sat down quietly, and told him why I was here.

"So, why are you here to see me today?"

"Well, um…I'm here to talk with you about what you said in class the other day."

I was talking quietly but loud enough so he could hear me. I was kind of nervous to be there, because I'm shy about meeting new people, but I wasn't too shy, because he was a pastor.

He gave me a story about when he was a freshman and felt alone, and wasn't sure if he belonged there or not.

"I was in the same boat you were, I was a lonely awkward freshman, didn't have many friends, missed home and didn't like my roommate. I survived that year and came back, and it was a thousand times better. I liked my roommate, I made friends, and didn't miss home as much, so trust me, it gets better."

I had no thoughts except; 'I will hold you to that.' But I just said okay.

Even though I only came to him specifically for one thing, he asked me more questions. Where are you from, why'd you pick this school, what are you majoring in, what classes are you taking? I answered every question, looking at him intently with every question he asked, and smiling after every one of them. The only way he made me not smile so much was when he asked me about my family.

I smiled at first, and then started crying a little, looking away because I hate crying in front of people, even my mom. I said it like it's not that big a deal, for me complaining to a pastor is like complaining to God himself.

"My life is okay, I guess; I just don't like it when my dad yells or hits my mom. He hit me a couple times, but never left a physical scar, it could be worse, I guess."

I said that all trying not to cry, quivering the whole time. It's true; I think my life isn't bad. Maybe because when I complain to my mom about my life she says things like, 'It's not that bad' or 'just don't think about it or worry about me'. So I try not to think that way. I guess my life isn't really that bad, other people have it way worse than me.

"I just wish my life was normal and I was happy," I said while crying.

He then directed me to a therapist on campus. She helped a little in my situation, but nobody can really help. What I want is a new life, and that is impossible. I asked for a therapist before, the front desk told me where to go and I got lost, so I said screw it, then my theology professor came to my rescue.

The thing I got out of most of what my therapist said was I'm a strong person for going through what I went through, and I shouldn't feel bad about anything. She did help me from the six months I talked with her. I walked around campus more with my head up, and even talked more. I loved talking to this guy, he helps me through a lot, and I look forward to talking with him.

I am not the type of person to complain to people, I feel bad and selfish complaining. For me, complaining is like saying I hate everything, and I will never be happy…I complain a lot, even though I hate it. I also feel like it's not other people's problem to worry or care about, unless it's a legit counselors, it's their job to listen to us complain.

2

FAILURE

In college you have to take a course on college life. Or at least at this college you have to; it's basically about how to adapt to college life, dorm life, managing homework, time management, moving away from home, etc. All the things I failed in.

In the first week, my professor talked to everyone about their experience at college so far, it was my turn.

"So, on a scale of one to ten, how would you say your college experience is going so far?"

"About a 7…"

"Really…? How or what can we do to make it better?"

"Um…I don't really know, friends…it's kind of personal?"

We'll talk about this later."

Oh great, I was kind of looking forward to our talk, although it never happened, he probably forgot about me (really wasn't that surprised).

I can say I like college way better than high school. The guys are cuter, I don't have 7 classes a day, and I can pick what time I want them to start, living on campus, parties, it's just amazing.

Although I've never been to a party or dated, my mom and other people just say you hear about the parties, but I hear nothing. See nobody. I like being invited places.

Like; "Hey, you want to come to this party tonight?"

"Sure, where is it?"

Oh no, that's not what happens in college. Apparently you hear it from other people, and somehow you know where it is. Well, one of my two friends I made at college told me she never heard anything at one of the football games. I wouldn't know because I have never been to a football game because I'm antisocial. Besides you have to drive to the fields, the one thing I don't like about this school.

Back to the guys, they look at me, but do they think I'm cute? I'm the type of person who doesn't know if someone is staring at you because they think you're pretty or ugly. Maybe it's the way I look at people, or look sad/mad most of the time, or is it because I really am ugly? Stop thinking, I'm here for an education.

No one ever asks me out, at this point I think it's me. My friend at home likes to play matchmaker and set me up with this guy once that only lasted three months. I broke up with him because we were too similar and our dates were silent and awkward. She still tries to set me up with people. According to my mom, they're scared to approach me because I'm too pretty. Thanks mom, I feel much better knowing that's the reason.

I only made a few close friends in my first semester and two of them are leaving. I made friends with one of my roommates who I thought I hated. I met the other two girls at a coloring contest I went to; now my roommate is taking a semester off, and the other is going back home to Virginia.

****

My first semester, I took this one class called Human Growth and Development. I liked it, but I was failing it.

After a few months of school there's a drop period where students can drop classes they don't want anymore. I didn't really have a choice but to drop the class, it was either that or I failed.

I managed to hide my grades from my mom for about 3 months.

"No mom, the professors haven't posted any grades yet"

As I just got my second F exam

I eventually had to tell her the adult decision I made to drop the class I liked that I was failing.

"Whelp, that's $300 down the drain."

My mom said when she heard the news.

"Well maybe if I wasted all that money why am I wasting more being at college, I'm not good enough anyway!"

"Well then maybe you should drop out, especially considering you failed a class and have a D in another."

Ah, the sound of a mother's encouragement. Gotta love her, though; I know she means well, most things she says out of anger, like me and my dad. I love them; I love them, huh…I love them.

So I dropped a class, and have a D in another, and the rest I have B's. The reason I dropped that class is because of softball, you need a certain GPA to play, and I wouldn't make the cut if I stayed in the Human Growth class. So I did it for softball. Even though I'm probably going to be a benchy like I was in high school. He played his favorites and I wasn't one of them, but hey maybe college will be different, highly doubt it, but maybe. If my high school had cuts in sports, I'd make nothing, and if I did make the team, I would probably be a benchy…which yes, I was. I was on the tennis team, bowling, cheerleading, and softball. Softball was the only sport I really liked, but my freaking coach would rarely play me.

I told my mom I probably was failing that class because I was in softball. It was too much, with other classes, this club I got sucked into starting, homework, sleep, practice, my state of mind, I was slowly losing it.

"Don't be stupid it's not softball, it's just because you're lazy, so quit…then why am I wasting all this money?"

Again with the money, this is why I spend so much time deciding whether to buy or do something or not. I wonder if it's worth it, I'm in college I shouldn't care about anything… or I should start caring? I mean I want to quit but I don't; if I quit I'll be bored, but if I stay I won't sleep, and have the fact of being a benchy. She's right, why waste money to sit on the bench?

Softball in high school ruined me. He NEVER played me, at least in a varsity game, but you can play in the JV games, that's more my level, a bunch of B.S. He didn't even play me on my senior night. I cried after that game, because I was the only senior he didn't play. He came to me after and said this line, "Hey, I'm sorry I didn't get a chance to play you. I guess I got so excited to beat them I forgot to play you. But I'll let you play the whole next game I PROMISE."

He didn't play me because I suck so badly. I felt that every game. I wouldn't wanna be the reason they lose. Hell, he played freshman before me, he even put the wrong picture of me in my senior yearbook, and he put this freaking freshmen who played one year! I guess you can't put someone in the yearbook that never got to play, so he got someone to look somewhat like me, so that was nice of him.

Anyway, it was the next game, he promised me playing time for the WHOLE game…yeah okay, what do you think happened? A ball was hit between right field and the second baseman. I was hit more in the right field direction, we both ran for the ball, and then collided into each other, both missing the ball. Of course, I got in trouble, even though neither of us called it (well, apparently she called it). It should have been my ball anyway because I had the better angle and she had to run backwards for it, but whatever. The midget second baseman told me to call it next time; I just gave her "the look" and mumbled words no one could hear. I didn't like much. She was the type of person that was "good at everything" and didn't seem to put much effort in things, and the one everyone liked, for what seemed like no apparent reason.

She annoyed me and I didn't even know why, you know, that one person who just irritates you for no valid reason. I guess because she played before me and she was "so good" when she missed the ball most of the time while batting. I swear no one ever likes me, but it's fine as always.

He benched me after that for the whole game, so much for his promise. I was so made I threw my water bottle against the wall and broke it. I was fuming, I was walking fast, lips pierced and angry, my eyes watering, breathing through my nose like a bull, everyone staring at me.

I was so furious, because he made a promise to me and broke it. I don't know why I expected the most out of him, the most out of anybody; I was hurt most of all, but it's FINE. I'm used to this shit. I don't get a second chance, and even if I do, I'll probably F it up, but little miss perfect gets unlimited chances. I just want to be someone's favorite for once, and given more than just a single chance or two to prove myself.

I was so angry I posted it on social media.

"I hate when people make promises and break them; I guess that's just the crappy world we live in." I told my mom.

"It's okay; I bet college will be better," is all she said.

"I don't even know if I wanna play anymore."

"Don't be stupid, what will you do then, sit around and get fat and lazy?"

"Um…study? Join band? Why waste all this money to sit on the bench?"

"Fine…then be a quitter."

Oh my geez, now I feel bad, you wonder why I think I'm stupid. Whenever I bring this conversation up, it's always like this. That's why I just stopped bringing it up and rarely talk at times, I'm done, done with all this, I just complain in my head now, which is worse…BUT IT'S FINE!

I guess softball did keep me busy. It was so much though, practicing every day and keeping up with the bowling club I started, and school, trying to be happy, I barely have time to sleep. I don't understand practicing when I know for sure I'm gonna be put on the bench…I guess to know I'll be a good backup.

Softball was the best when I was in t-ball and I didn't know what disappointment was; everyone got to play, I had friends, and the coaches were great. The coaches complimented us when I did something good, and would give encouragement and advice when we did something wrong.

Every coach I had had a daughter on the team though, because who else would coach a team besides someone's dad? I would make sure to make friends with her because that would mean the coach would like me, even though I sucked in the field, I was great at bat. I hit the winning hit once and that felt so good, everyone hugged me, even the coaches, it was the best feeling, plus I got the game ball and a free slice of pizza.

I had no doubt there were favorites, especially the coach's daughter, but it is his daughter, so I couldn't really blame them for liking their own kid.

When I was in sixth grade, I found out the district team I've been playing on for years isn't a team anymore. So I and my mom looked for a different team to play for. We started looking for travel softball teams rather than district teams, since those are the "best" and "more advanced" teams to be on. Because they're more competitive and you have to try out and actually be good…that was the problem, I was average. The only travel teams I could get on were the B teams, which were lower than the A teams (obviously). They made us try out even though we made the team anyway, and they aren't as competitive as the A team, I think I liked it better that way anyway, the less competitive the better.

The A teams were the best of the best, and I wasn't the best, and I knew it. I tried out for an A team once, and went home crying. The pitching was faster, the balls were hit harder. You had to pay attention at all times and make little to no mistakes. It was rough. I missed most of the balls hit to me, and couldn't hit any ball, I felt so little, meanwhile other girls caught everything and hit "dingers".

Well, I and my mom later found out the coach who used to coach the district games made a travel team, with all the girls I used to play with. My mom called him up to ask if I can try out.

"Oh, sorry we have enough people on our team and only accept people that played with us before for district ball."

Um…okay, I played with you for six years, I know your bitchy daughter, and can I at least try out? Nope. Sorry, we're full, no room for me. I can't believe he never told me about his travel team, and EVERYONE from the district team was on the team. Even a few girls who weren't on the team before they became travel ball; I thought he only accepted people who played with him before? Two years that he went without telling us. I'm really not surprised no one told us, and I am fine, because softball slowly became a part of my anxiety.

I loved going home after a long day of baseball, getting a good hit, my teammates and crowd cheering me on, the high fives I would get from my teammates and coaches. Then we'd get food at the old wooden concession stand, the smell of pizza and nachos, and bees trying to get our food. That feeling is gone now, since I'm not on his team anymore and apparently never played with him before. I bet he didn't want me on his team because he thought I sucked, well screw you Jim, I don't want to be on your team anyway, with your daughter, screw you and her. I'm on this other cool team cooler than yours.

She really did nothing wrong. She's just that person you dislike for no good reason. It was just that she was the coach's daughter, had more friends, probably a normal life, a nice figure, and seemed to stuck up to talk to anyone who didn't play softball. She did have the same name as me so that was cool.

I loved going home after a good day of softball. But other times I thought, can I go somewhere else with my friends, to a "normal" family where their dad isn't scary looking and probably not yelling? There was no other place to go other than home, yes I had friends on the team, but we never really hung out after games, we would just all have fun during games and practice. I hated going home, hearing my dad in one of his moods again. Then I'd go in my room and cry in my bed. I felt like I couldn't do anything around the house like play with the dog or watch TV. I would have the urge to tiptoe everywhere, God forbid if we were too loud, he'd get angry.

I did like going home when he was in a good mood. My mom would tell him what happened, he would tell me I did a good job, and then I would go back to my room in a good mood. I would usually have my mom say something to him first, so I could feel him out to see what mood he was in. If he responded in an angry voice I wouldn't say anything. If he responded in a soft, calm voice, I would talk to him. Wow, I was only ten-years-old and had to worry about going home; needing to feel my dad out to see what mood he was in. I was honestly scared of my dad sometimes, when he would yell; he'd tighten his upper lip over his little teeth as he screamed at us. He looked murderous that way, and when he'd hit my mom, it would be like a football play, but with loud stomping through the house, the sound of screaming and skin slapping on skin.

****

I know I have to go to college, I just don't think I'm good enough. I don't even know what I want to do with my life yet; do I want to be a teacher…a scientist…a biologist? I think about this all the time, even during classes. It's why I do so badly probably. Even when I think I know my career, I don't; I would space out in class and think about my future, my past life, other people's life, there was so much.

When I was deciding on a school, I literally had a dream I went where I am now…then I woke up and decided to go here. I was so happy. In my dream I could see the brick walls I see now, and everyone was nice, like they are now, I just wish I didn't feel as lonely.

I had no doubt, it was a sign, because I really like this school (I just wish I had more friends, but that's more of a me-problem than the school's problem).

My dream job was to be a lawyer, but you have to be really smart for that, and it takes forever to become one. By the time I graduate I'll be in a lot of debt, and what if I don't get a job, or I'm a crappy lawyer? I know colleges help you look for jobs, but what if they can't find one for me?

It takes a lot to make your potential dreams come true, so they almost always stay dreams.

****

When I was a senior in high school, I was reading a book; it was so good I couldn't put it down. Hanging on to every detail, I then conjured up this crazy idea I could write a book. That's what I'll do with my life, become an author. I sort of had a plan. I'd write two pages a day, that'll have me with enough pages for a book in about three months; I just don't know what to write about, my life, or where to start?

I could thank and say this person was my inspiration, my super cool and chill band teacher who read this book that resembled my life. Yes, he read a book to us in high school, but it was more of a short devotional reading.

His book was amazing, it was about his life and how he overcame his struggles, it's also kind of like my life. As he read the book to us, I took in the words and stuck to them, picturing what the guy went through, comparing everything to my personal life. He would say depressing things like I would say, complain like I would, do things like I would, and was he me? Obviously not, but I knew I wanted to write like him.

I think I have enough experience to write a book, I mean, I read books, pay attention in and to English. Yes, I'm going to write a book, but not tell anyone so they won't make fun of me, and so they can be surprised I wrote a book.

I told my mom when I was young, I want to sing, maybe be like Taylor Swift, go into a studio and play them my track.

"Hey mom, will you take me to Nashville, if I write a good song?"

"Sure."

"Cool, but don't tell anyone"

My mom can't keep anything a secret.

The next day in church my mom told my aunt without telling me. We were singing a hymn and they both just glanced at me.

"I wanted to see if you were singing." She whispered.

Dang, now people know, and I'm embarrassed. I went home and recorded myself with my "good" singing voice, turns out it wasn't that good; I sounded like, well I can't even explain it. It was just awful. I can cross that off my dream list. Maybe I can be the Taylor Swift who writes books, putting her songs in book form.

But I can write a book, I swear. I would stress about it, imagining how I would thank everyone, what I would say on talk shows. I was getting way ahead of myself, wondering when a good time to start would be. I would also think of it not being good, like what if they read it at comedy shows it's so bad, 'worst book ever'. Well, at least I'll be famous for something, right? If college fails, I got a potential back up at least.

Next thing I knew it was freshman year of college and I had nothing, so much for a backup. I would write things down in a journal, but what's the use, it probably won't even be that good because nothing I do is good.

3

FRIENDS

A friend is a person you can tell anything to; trust them to keep a secret. My mom is the only exception; I love her but she can't keep a secret, like I said about me singing.

She usually tells my dad what I tell her, and that causes most arguments.

"I think we should've got the basement redone instead of the backyard, it raises the price of the house more, but don't tell dad I don't want him to get mad."

"Okay."

"Well now, we gotta finish the backyard. We already spent this much money on it, I barely have money for the yard." My dad would say, after my mom tells him what I said. I'm done talking.

Then why spend the money? The yard was fine how it was; it looks prettier though I'd have to admit. I'm gonna shoot myself, now he's yelling about that. I remember saying something about segregation to my mom and told her not to tell dad, what does she do? She tells my dad. I just don't tell him stuff because he over-thinks it and gets mad, especially about the news and politics, I know where my over-thinking comes from now.

"What a world we live in, it's sad." He always says.

Yes, we live in a screwed up world, but what can we do? There's only so much we can do, like volunteering in one place can make a huge difference? That's usually when I go to my room.

I would never talk about religion with him, we tried that on a ski trip once, and it didn't go so hot. My dad gets most of his information from when he was a kid, and from the history channel, which is false sometimes. I'm pretty sure he believes, although he has damned God before and us, so I don't know for sure, but I think he believes in a higher power.

****

I had mostly band friends in high school, weird, awkward, band friends. Most of them were depressed and socially awkward like me; I liked them because they didn't seem to judge me, or if they did, they accepted me for me.

Freshman year in high school, I met this intimidating black girl in my math class, we were in groups together. She was a little taller than me, wearing dark clothes, glasses, and was bigger than me, especially her chest (not jealous…).

I was in a group of four with the one intimidating girl, a short, pretty black girl, and a black guy, and me. The teacher handed out a piece of paper, one of the questions was.

"How do you know your grade?"

And I put, "I don't worry about it."

Yep, that was the start. The intimidating black girl looked at my paper and started laughing. She told the rest of the group, they all looked at my paper and started laughing. Then I did, they were saying they can't believe I wrote that, but it was true, I didn't worry about my grades then, I guess I am funny.

After the teacher collected them, she read them out loud.

"I was disappointed at some of your responses; some of you put things like 'I don't check them' or 'I don't worry about it'."

My section busted out laughing again, including me, and that's how I got my name, and made my first friend. The intimidating girl and I were in the same math class all 3 years I took math. We were best buds. I even remember this one time, I was staring intently at the board, and she poked me in the neck softly with her pencil. I freaked out and jumped out of my seat, she started dying of laughter, then I did too, we still laugh about it till this day.

She was like a bodyguard to people, if she found out somebody she liked was getting bullied or teased by someone else, she would tell the person bugging them to flick off.

I loved them even though they were weird. I told my mom about them, and she met them a few times, when they would leave she'd tell me.

"Can't you find some normal friends? This is why you don't have a boyfriend because you hang around with weirdoes."

She was mostly joking

"I don't care, I like them, and I don't even want a boyfriend right now".

Which was a little white lie

My mom likes my friends; she just thinks they're weird. She likes them even more since I had a fight with my brother's wife's sister, who was my so-called best friend. Plus, I'd honestly rather have friends than a boyfriend, anyway (another little white lie).

* * *

My brother had a girlfriend when he was a junior in high school; they dated for about seven years before they got married. I was in seventh grade at the time when they started dating, and so was her sister.

They introduced us in seventh grade, but we didn't hang out much. We were very different, she was cool and wore makeup, I was lame and wore no makeup, and she also had a few boyfriends in her time, unlike me.

I secretly wanted to be like her; she did her makeup nice, dressed nice, cute dimples; got straight A's, had boyfriends before, and was way cooler than me. The main reason she was cooler than me is she wasn't awkward like me. She always knew how to say things, I always thought she was a little stuck up and rude back then though, but things changed about sophomore year, then changed again when she punched me.

Sophomore year, I started wearing makeup and got an iPhone; I finally started to feel normal. She was great at math, and even got an award for it, meanwhile I got a D in algebra. She got A's and B's and I got mostly C's, seriously what was I good at?

I tried almost every sport in high school: tennis, softball, bowling, and cheer. Well, I wasn't peppy enough to be a cheerleader. I was an alternate in case any one got hurt. I didn't know any gymnastics like the others, and I just wasn't that good. So that only lasted a year. I was okay at tennis, and scored an average of 90 in bowling. Softball is the only sport I'm really decent at and understand it completely, though I'm not the best of the best, like that one midget. I only made the teams because they had no cuts, if they did, I probably would've made none, well, maybe softball. I wanted to try out for volleyball, but my mom told me it's really competitive and I wouldn't make the team, but I could still try out. Well now I lost my confidence in that, so no. She told me the same thing with bowling and tennis.

"You suck at bowling."

"You wanna join tennis?!?"

"Volleyball is really competitive; don't be upset if you don't make the team."

Okay, she didn't exactly say I wouldn't make the team, but she implied it, therefore lowering my self-esteem. The only reason I joined tennis and bowling was my weird but awesome friends were on tennis, and my "so called friend", was on bowling. I loved those sports, even if I wasn't the best.

My "so called friend", really came to me junior year of high school. She lost her boyfriend and her other friends, so I guess she came to me. I don't know if she was just using me, but I needed a "normal" friend and her sister was my brother's wife, so I might as well get to know her more. We had a year full of it.

She was a good friend nonetheless; she listened to me and offered me to stay with her if things got bad. I also liked hanging out with her and these other chill guys from our school, we would mostly play games, get ice cream or food, and joke around, and sometimes drink.

I really missed her when I went off to college. She taught me so much; I would pick up on things she does and try to be more like her and less awkward. I would still act somewhat like me, just not as awkward, I'm still awkward just not as bad…I think. She was my best friend (thanks to my brother).

She does do a lot of things I didn't like, like sleeping with a lot of guys, making me stay out really late, making me lie to my mom. She tries to control me, like when I say I can't do things or don't want to. She tries to get me to do it, or gets mad when I don't. She once got mad at me because my mom gives me a curfew and her mom doesn't, so we got into this huge argument; it's either her way or hell breaks loose.

She needs some chill, or has too much of it. Either way I need sleep. Yeah we have fun, but my mom is about to kill me right now, and I need to go home and eat my vegetables and not go on my third day of fast food.

I cried the whole day after because I made my mom worry about me. I was so mad at my friend; she wants everyone to go her way. I get she likes to have fun but some things are too much, like going downtown at four am, going to Chicago from four am. to sunrise. That's hella dangerous, especially that a lot of crime happens down there, rather than where I live. Thank God we lived, and didn't get abducted by the two random guys we were with.

She told me she tells her mom she's depressed, so her mom lets her do whatever, and she told me to say the same thing to my mom. Okay I'll tell her, but she still won't let me out; I don't like having her worry or be mad at me, I like telling her the truth, and so does she. My "so called friend" honestly bugs me sometimes. Just because she wants only what she wants. She gets mad when she doesn't get her way. I feel like she uses me just sometimes just because she never started talking to me since her boyfriend left, and she lost her other friend. If she says I have no friends, how come she keeps texting me and getting me to do stuff with her, even when I say no? She honestly needs to grow up. But, we found, or I found ways to cope with her, and we do have fun when we're together, even though we may fight at times.

I don't think we'll ever be friends since the big fight, it was the first real fight we had. It all happened when we were on vacation, and I said I miss back home.

"Why do you miss home so much, you don't do anything there?"

"Yes I do, why do you say that?"

"Well it's true you have no friends and you do nothing, I have a job and have friends!"

I should've punched her right there, but I just called her a bitch…and then she punched me. I never thought she would've actually punched me, because she was driving and we were friends, nope, she slammed on the brakes and punched me in the face. I was full of shock and adrenaline after she punched me. I got up from my seat and punched her as hard as I could. We started fighting like girls, just slapping each other and weak punching. She pulled me by my sweatshirt and my hair, held me close to her, and said she would kill me. When I finally got her to let go, I said she needed stronger meds and that she's a psycho and a bad sister. I would've gotten out of the car when she told me too but we were in the middle of a cornfield in North Carolina, where there are bears.

The next day, I went home with my brother and his wife, they didn't really want to drive me home but they had no choice.

When we finally got back to the cabin, my "so called friend" told her mom I punched her first, which is a total lie, but whatever. I just cried…because I think we ended our friendship, even if I was a skeptic to begin with.

Her mom came down to the lake to talk to both of us, because I was sitting on the dock and she was up stairs. She was mostly shocked because we did this on vacation and "ruined" it. I told her mom how her daughter punched me first and how she wanted to kill me, which my "so called friend" of course denied them both. First off, I hate lying and why would I make something up like that? I remember that day still like it was yesterday, and every time I think of it, I get all worked up. I just hope I left a mark on her face like she did mine; I did rip her stupid earring out.

I was done with her, she was never my friend, or she was a damn good fake one at that.

This of course never happened last year when I went. I guess she got sick of me by then, invite one of the many guys you slept with next time. I hope you guys get eaten by a bear, you deserve it. Nah, that's too mean. I'm just reeealy mad at her and will be for a while.

She didn't act like a fake friend, so I don't really know what her problem was? She did have anxiety and depression, worse than me. I would try to be there for her as much as I could.

So I guess nobody knows the real story except me and God, because she lied to everyone and she's honestly second-guessing me sometimes. Did I really hit her first? No, because why would I hit her when she's driving, and I'm not like that. I don't like her at this moment, and neither does my family, they were as pissed as I was.

When I got home back in Illinois, all I could think about was getting back at her. I wanted to report what she did to the police, I had evidence, my bruised nose and eye, and I saw nothing on her fat face. Everybody said to just let it go and that they couldn't do anything because it happened two days ago and it was out of state. But I was sure they could do something, hell she assaulted me and threatened to kill me, and I was kind of scared!

Okay, that won't fly, so I emailed mental hospitals to send her back there.

"Hello,

I would like to refer my friend in here, she has behavioral problems, and assaulted me the other day, and I am concerned for her well-being, please get back to me.

Sincerely,

****

They emailed back explaining what they do there to help people like her, a lot of therapy. I'm actually surprised they emailed me back.

I thought of ways to get revenge without getting in trouble or cause or retaliation, because violating her car would lead in retaliation or it could get me in trouble. So I gave her number to telemarketers. I gave her number to this one gay therapy place; it's funny because she's not gay. She at least won't know who did it to her.

It's been a week now and my blood is finally simmering down, who needs her, not me that's who. I'll just listen to my music and watch TV, like really nothing has changed; at least I'm not out all night, keeping my parents awake.

I told the chief of police that I find one of their cadets not suitable for the job, because she punched me in the face and threatened to kill me. He responded by saying I was describing an assault and needed to file a police report. I didn't want to do that because it would start a whole other big mess, so I just said okay and thank you for your time. At least I got her before she got me. Emailing him first was a good idea, so if she says anything to the chief, I already told him first, therefore he should believe me if anything goes down. I need to stop.

At least I got real friends, friends who I know won't punch me in the face and I love more. Friends who I told this story to cheered me up, taking my side. Friends who don't lie to me, friends who hate her as much as I do, real friends, they may be quirky, but I love them. I could go on and complain about her, but I shall learn to let go to make me happier, and just worry about me and live my life.

The thing that really made me snap at her was when she said I do nothing with my life and have no friends. That made me think, and I really kind of don't do much or have that many friends. I usually sleep till late and watch TV all day, it is kind of sad. She also knows what a loser I was at college. I would complain to her how I have no friends and how I don't like college. Damn, why would I say that to her, and why would she say it back to me, like her life is so much more amazing? She's honestly still a child, on the way home with my brother, she sent Snapchats to me of people saying they're not my friend, so childish. At least I have real friends, and not guys who use me just for sex. She's good at making people feel like shit I'll give her that. It's bad enough I got my family doing that.

Like my family and friends said, you don't need people like her in your life; she's toxic and a user. She won't go anywhere in life if she keeps treating people like she does. You're better and nicer than her.

I just wonder if she thinks about me like I think about her. Is she really thriving more than me? Does she feel guilty for what she did? Does she miss me? Does she do more fun stuff than me? Does she still belittle me? Does she miss the stuff we did together? Does she tell her friends how she bet my ass? Is this keeping her from living like it is me? I'll think about the situation sometimes. And get pissed all over again and want to smack her. It sucks that this happened, because I think about how we were really good friends at one time, we'd have sleepovers, joke around together, and basically act like sisters. This irritates me. Whatever, I guess she wasn't meant to be in my life, maybe we'll make up in the future, we are kind of family. I need to let this go. She's no real friend, and just uses people, just shows how your best friend can betray you; besides, I'd rather have one real friend than ten fake friends who just use you.

Right after our fight, I saw this article on Facebook that said your best friends are the ones you fight with the most. It got me thinking…I wasn't thinking so much that I would text her, but it got me thinking. We'll probably end up being friends again, we just need a break.

****

As I stated before, I had a total of three best friends at college, *real* friends, my roommate, and these girls I met at a coloring contest. When the second semester started I lost two of them. One took a semester off and the other moved back to Virginia. At least I still have one friend, and do fun stuff with my other roommate who I never really talked to before since my other roommate.

My roommate and I were best buds, the roommate I didn't know if I would like, I ended up liking (but then of course she left.) We would play pool when we were bored and didn't feel like doing homework. We would joke around, laugh a lot, make comments while watching TV, and quote funny videos. We had so much fun and laughed until we cried. Although she did remind me of my dad at times, she would get mad at me about little stupid things; we would argue, then forget about it and joke about it the next day. I guess this is normal in all relationships?

We once argued about suicide, during a floor event, so everybody heard, but obviously didn't bother to care because they just listened and didn't do anything, probably too shocked to say anything.

"Suicide is selfish and you only care about yourself when you do it," she said.

"That's not always true, some people can't help it."

And we would go back and forth about it, sometimes she would just cut me off and say things like 'exactly my point you don't have one', which made my blood boil. She was kind of right in a way suicide does seem selfish, but yet, some people can't help it; it's a very serious issue most people struggle with. I see where she's coming from though. Someone escaping life because they can't handle it, they can handle it, but they just don't want to. So they escape, it seems pretty selfish if you really think about it; there are a lot of things that come into play here.

We never talked about that conversation again, except at the end of the year when we argued about it again for some reason. At the end, we admitted we both like arguing. It is true, because we get things off our chests and shout out our thoughts, no wonder my dad loves it so much.

On the very last day of our first semester me, my roommate and my other friend stayed up all night, I will never do that again. I almost made it, but fell asleep at like 5 am, and felt sick because I was so tired. My roommate was used to it because she stayed up all night anyway. I don't even know what exactly we talked about.

It was about four o'clock in the morning before I passed out, and the one thing I remembered talking about was our deep conversation about how we thrived this year. And though it may not seem like I did, I did, at least a little. We all said how it was great we all met each other, and it honestly was, I grew a lot because of them, and I hope to grow more.

4

THE YEAR

It was the first day of my second semester, I texted my one best friend who's still here that I'm here on campus, oh no, she's not responding. The next day I texted her to go to lunch with me…still, there was no answer.

"Hello? Where are you?!"

Nothing, I was losing hope, thinking she left too. I started asking people she talked to if they'd seen her; they said they didn't hear from her. I wondered if she did leave. But she said she was coming back?! Maybe she couldn't afford it, and the first semester was too much? Whelp, there goes my other friend, this year sucks so far, '2020 will definitely be my year', nah I don't really care anymore, I'm just trying to survive now.

I kind of miss high school at this point. I had more friends, better food, my parents, and my dog. I thought about transferring or dropping out so many times, but what would I do if I drop out? My mom said I would have to go to community college, if I transfer. Community college to me wasn't a "real" college (according to my parents and society as well). There are so many positive influences in my life.

If I drop out, I won't get a good job…this is so stressful! I thought about the only easy solution, ending it. The only reason I won't is because I wouldn't do that to my family and friends, and I don't know where I'll go, Heaven or Hell- nobody knows, not even pastors…and it's "selfish."

To make things worse, I need another credit to be full time and be able to graduate on time. I had enough during break, but they dropped everyone in the math course I was going to take, because the professor died…so they kicked everyone out of that course.

I tried to work things out with my advisor.

"Well why can't I just stick with twelve credits?"

"I would really rather have you take another class, so you could be caught up, and not have trouble with graduation."

I don't understand why I couldn't keep my twelve and just take more credits next year to catch up. I didn't want to add another class because I thought it would be hard with softball. Plus, I had to switch my whole freaking schedule around…but I'll do what my college advisor says, he does make the big bucks.

Whelp, I got my stupid math class in, fifteen credits…if I fail, I'm dropping out. This is too much, I should forget writing a book because it's never gonna happen, I'll just add that to my stress level and dreams that will never come true.

At least I found my one and only friend on campus… after a week of being alone; she came back late because of something I guess with her financial aid.

Good. Everything is fine now, and I feel less alone. We talked about how our breaks and holidays went. After we talked about our breaks and how nothing exciting happened, we went to the store nearby and got some groceries. I of course got stuff I didn't need, like cake and frosting…I had a craving, ate some, and threw it away the next day. I really need to be better with money.

I loved her, she was so cute and had a positive attitude about things, which I really needed, she shaped me for the better, and made me be more outgoing and talkative to people. During break, I really missed our walks downtown with her and walking to Taco Bell and Starbucks. We loved to walk places, even in freezing weather; we would walk and talk when we wanted to avoid actual work. She was a great friend, and I knew we'd never fight, and we'd be friends for a long time…we did fight, but made up, eventually. I felt comfortable around her, which I can't say for everyone.

****

Great, I ate the cake- in-a cup, and now I'm wide awake. It was 10 O'clock by this time. I have to get up early and travel to this funeral all the way in Iowa. I'm not complaining I have to go, just that I hate sleeping sitting up in a seat, and I need to go to bed now but can't.

Before the first day of second semester started, this girl on the softball team died in her dorm room. I guess she didn't take her medication for her diabetes…My little school was even on the news. It's sweet that we're going to the funeral. I think it's nice we're all going, it's just, I didn't know her all that well, and I'd feel kind of misplaced going, also I didn't fit in with those girls. I did talk to her once, and she was a good softball player; I still loved her, even though I barely knew her. It's crazy how much you think about life when you hear someone else's life was cut short.

This may sound strange, but why am I a little jealous? Not that she died, but of how many people came to her memorial at school, and cried for her. I wondered if people would do that if I died, did they all even know her, or are they just going to pay respects? I need to get these thoughts out of my head, I shouldn't think this way, why am I thinking this way, and I can't be the only one who thinks this way? There must be at least another person as stupidly jealous as I am.

All the people who spoke for her said she always had a smile on her face, and was in a great mood, I never noticed…but yet again, we never really talked. She was a nice person, from that one interaction I had with her on that one night. I played bingo with her this night, but she didn't really talk to me; she was really soft-spoken, at least to me. I wondered how many friends she really had, how her family life was, was she a generally happy person, because she seemed kind of sad to me.

I mostly thought of her parents and brothers. When we went to the funeral; a lady who I think was her grandma was bawling her eyes out, more than her parents were. I tried to get sad, but I didn't know her that well, which made me feel worse. It must be really hard losing someone that young, though I tried hard to imagine, all I know is it's literally heart breaking. Was she really close to her family? Did she do a lot of stuff with her mom? Did she have a good relationship with her dad? I kept thinking of these scenarios with her not in the picture. How different it would be without her, her parents having to go on without her, looking in her empty room, things that remind them of her. I think of how my mom would be if I was gone. It makes me tear up. I get sad thinking of the fact she was gone so soon, reminiscing of the news interview of her death and the memorial service, I didn't even get to know her. Nonetheless, I love her and will remember her and her family forever.

I don't mean to sound like a bitch, but I kind of did, being envious of someone who died a tragic death…so bizarre. I thought, what's the big deal, let's move on? But I say that without thinking, knowing it takes time, and as a school we should honor her in respect and always remember her. It was an extremely shocking and unexpected event that happened. I couldn't stop thinking about it. Not many people die in college, and if they do, it's tremendously sad. I loved her like a sister in Christ, I guess. I feel like I should be more affected by her death, but I'm not so much, I mean I am, just not as much as say her parents. I'm just a person who is jealous of how much she is loved, and wish I felt the same…I feel so selfish.

I want to leave a legacy when I leave. I want people to like me; know who I really am, get to know me. I feel like people don't. It would maybe help if I talked to them more. But I'm the type of person who thinks if you don't come to me, you must not want to talk to me, and I'm shy and awkward. I think I gave up trying at this point, nice right? I'm 18, and I give up. Let them come to me if they really want to talk, I'll talk back I promise (I should get a shirt that says that).

My mom told me to get their numbers to hang out with them, but what if they don't want my number? If a person wants to hang out with me more or talk with me, they'll ask me for my number…so I wait, with an approachable look on my face so people talk to be…but nothing.

Geez, why am I like this? I shout to God hoping he'll hear me. 'Fix me, please!' Part of me thinks I'll never be fixed, and nobody can fix me except God. That's why I don't seek help, what can they do? I need to work on myself, starting with myself.

"I know you hear me! I want to feel your presence; I want to know I am loved!"

Great, the only person that can fix me can't verbally speak to me, maybe through others, but I can barely hear them. The end can't come soon enough…At least I have my one friend who helps a bit, she'll tell me to stay positive, but that can only help so much.

I've been talking to my one friend from high school, who hates college as much as I do. Okay, I don't HATE College…It's just hard and exhausting. We'll stay on the phone for hours, talking about how different things are, and how we hate our roommates; something about someone else complaining about something you are too, makes you not feel alone.

I forgot to mention Christmas, a great holiday right? Maybe for the meaning but that's about it. About every Christmas I feel bad about the money, and my dad complains about what he got, he's like a little kid.

"This is too small."

"This is too big."

"You can't buy anything right."

"Great now we gotta return it/ ship it back."

I feel bad for my mom, she just has a smile on her face saying things like; "yeah, yeah, I messed up". I can tell it's a fake smile. She listens to him, inspecting every little thing, with thoughts in her mind that she messed up…than I put a smile on my face, and putting more Baileys in my coffee.

"Well this is the wrong part for the motorcycle, yeah, this will never fit, I should've approved of it, now we gotta ship it back, and you can't get anything right."

* Fake laughter*

I'm thinking, so what's the big freaking deal, ship it back, what will it take like two-to-three business days? You don't race until the spring anyway, and it's winter now.

I don't understand why he wants that stuff anyway, he never goes anymore. He says because he's always tired, when the real reason is that my brother's wife goes and he doesn't like her that much. It's not that he hates her, it's just she's not the most social person, and can come off as unfriendly at times…but that's all women. I completely understand though. She probably gets moody because she has diabetes. One of the side effects is stubbornness, well it's not an actual side effect but when your blood sugar goes real high or low, the person's behavior can change. Out of all people, I can't believe he doesn't understand, because he gets that way too, even worse than her.

She can be really clingy to my brother sometimes, too. It's like she wants to be with him 24/7. Or like my dad wants to be with my mom 24/7 (It seems like they hate each other, but I guess they don't… I stop asking things.) My dad complains how he can never hang out with just them, too. He either leaves them alone, or has to deal with both of them, which he hates; I honestly don't know what he likes anymore.

My dad and even my mom sometimes, say how difficult she can be. I'm always like, well it's understandable she's like this, she has diabetes and her dad's kind of an ass (her family is screwed up like ours, man can we pick 'em). I try to see the way other people are, like her being clingy and difficult at times is just how her life was growing up (I'll understand others, but I won't understand myself).

"How was dinner?" My dad asked us.

"She was in one of her moods today."

"Well, that's because she's probably tired from work."

"Why do you always have to stick up for her?"

"I'm leaving you two to work this out, I'm sorry I asked!" My dad stormed off. "I'm tired of this shit!"

Then she gave me the look saying, 'now, look what you did.' Why is it always my fault, like I should know what triggers my dad? (I guess I really should by now). He was literally fine when asking us how dinner was, my mom yelled at me, and then my dad got mad and stormed off. This is why I don't talk.

She did call my mom a bitch one time, but she apologized for it eventually. We all say things out of anger, my dad says he hates me, which I think is true sometimes, but that's beside the point. I said I wanted to kill someone one time, and it got me expelled, even after I apologized; words can get you in trouble sometimes.

She also has depression, and that has side effects too, being happy one second and sad the next. It's not like you ask for depression, it comes at random times sometimes even, and surprises you, and you may not know something will depress you until it does. Depression sucks, I don't know exactly what she goes through, but I understand why she gets moody, that's why I stick up for her most of the time, I can relate. Depression can make you not want to talk for days…and we just have to figure out ways to deal with this and "move on".

You can't really ever move on from certain things, you always have the memory of it; we may move on from things, but they have shaped us all to who we are today. Maybe she's like me, jealous of other people's lives. We know we can't change it, and that's mainly what depresses us, the fact we can't change what happened; maybe she sees resemblances she doesn't want to see?

I'm really, or was, good friends with her sister, she has depression too, all my friends do, and man can I really pick em too. She would ask me how my day is, I complain to her and she complains to me, that's basically it. I tried to make her feel better one time when she was crying, and it backfired, she got a ticket and was crying.

"It's okay, it'll be fine."

"No, it really won't, I pay for school, my dog, my car, and now I got a ticket."

The ticket was sixty dollars, it's not like four hundred or more, whatever, and I'll never understand money issues.

"Maybe I'll be like you and just rely on others to drive me places and use up their gas."

She said out of anger (I told myself), I was kind of offended; this is what I get for trying to help. Yes, I do rely on others, because they say they don't mind driving me around. I don't want to waste my gas, and my mom says not to be driving around because it's technically not my car. I think of that now every time someone drives me places, and it makes me feel bad.

****

My winter break was like a month and two weeks long, so I was ready to go back to school…until I actually got back. School was already stressful, especially because I had to add another class to "fill my credits." I had enough credits to begin with, but had to have another one to not be behind. I don't understand why I couldn't just take more next year; I would have more time because I probably wouldn't play softball…but whatever.

So after stressing about that, from having only one class on Thursday to having three per day, I was not that happy. But it's whatever I guess.

I was stressed from my math class, because I didn't really know if I was doing the problems right, or how to submit them online. My biology lab sucked, I didn't really know what I was doing, was really slow at getting the material…but would somehow make it through. Maybe I really am slow, or have ADHD or something? I bombed my communication speech; I rehearsed what I was going to say, but panicked. I had an outline and everything, I just didn't practice enough I guess.

"I am like a book, you need to read me to know me…um, and yeah that's pretty much it."

It was a speech, and you had to say "I am like a…", so I chose a book, and got all these facts why I am like a book. I practiced it in my room a little. I was confident about it, and got a coffee to perk me up. I stood up in class and talked there for about a minute when it was supposed to be five minutes, paused, got nervous, and then walked back with my head down and face red. I hate giving a speech and pausing, having complete silence, then everything is ruined, my heart races, and I forget what I have to say. I got a C on it, not bad, but not great either, average, which is no surprise. It didn't help I hate speeches and my voice whenever I speak. My professor recorded the speeches and handed them to us…I watched ten seconds of it, closed my computer, and then cried; at least I didn't fail.

5

CONFIDENCE

Depression makes you not want to get out of bed, sometimes. It makes your vision seem foggy and gloomy. It's not looking depressed but still being depressed. It makes you tired even though you've slept twelve hours. It's getting mad for no good reason. It's the wanting to do something but too depressed and lazy to do anything. It's getting sad over little things. It's over-thinking, thinking people don't like you, it completely sucks…you can have good days and bad days, you could even die from depression, believe it or not, but confidence is key! The guy I've been talking to sent me an email saying if I'd like to meet with him and talk. I went to his office, and he asked me how I was doing.

"So, how are you?"

"Okay, I guess."

"How's back home?"

"Okay, I guess."

Everything was okay to me, it's not horrible, but could be better, so I was confident of that.

"I just wish I had more friends. I try to be social but it doesn't seem to be working well, I just wish I can make friends easily, like others that I see, and not be so awkward and shy."

He basically said what my mom said, force yourself to go to social events, no matter how awkward it may feel for you, and get yourself to talk to people. I try, but I feel too awkward, like I shouldn't be there…I compare myself to others too much and lower my self-esteem; I'm my biggest enemy. I need confidence; I feel like other people don't care what I have to say, so what's the point in talking? Even if they are laughing with you and respond to you…is it genuine?

"Get them to talk about themselves, people love talking about themselves," he says.

Well, the problem with that is…I don't care most of the time… or they'll probably think I'm stalking them and that I'm weird, "where are you from? What grade are you in? What are you studying? How many siblings do you have?" People don't get to know me, so why should I get to know them? Also don't want to be the person that asks too many questions.

My one friend and I went on this weekend-long retreat thing during second semester. I felt awkward the majority of the trip; I didn't wanna play the games they had, because that would involve meeting new people, which I'm obviously not that great at. When I got back to school, I regretted not playing the games they had, and should've put myself out there more…I always get this way! I should've done this, I should've done that…oh well, it happened (or didn't) time to move on…if only. I'm really not that awkward, it's just all in my head. Why am I like this? It's my stupid mind that makes me feel this way. Maybe I'm not even that awkward…or my awkwardness is what people like about me. I guess I'll never know that unless I talk to people.

I just need to accept myself…sometimes I say YOLO (You Only Live Once) and not care what people think of me, and other times I care too much. My mood changes a lot. If I'm thinking of doing something risky, like talking to new people or dancing, I have to think about it a lot. I have to make myself do it; to be in the mood to let myself loose. What makes me do things is not caring what others think of me, and to just have fun, and it really does work. At least I don't go back regretting not doing something I wanted or should do, and beat myself up for not doing certain things. I actually do love talking to new people; I'm just scared for some reason. Who cares what others think? Just have fun, life's too short.

****

College made me so much more suicidal than I already was (good first sentence). The stress of school, being away from home, not having many friends, not getting good grades, and comparing myself to others… My brain hurts. Other people are probably more outgoing, because their family life was more "normal" than mine. Most people probably get good grades because their family life was normal. Most people probably make more friends because their family life is normal. Most people probably live life and say YOLO. I think most of the reason I'm like this, is because my dad made me feel insecure, and I eventually just gave up trying and talking. That way I know for a fact I won't get hurt…but I still do, even more so probably because I don't talk. What really bugs me is when my dad does these things, and doesn't apologize for it and acts perfectly normal the day after his little tantrums. I used to ignore him until I got the long awaited apology that never came…but I don't expect anything anymore, he never apologizes, and I feel bad ignoring my dad. I gave up already, which is actually less stressful, not expecting things and just going with whatever.

I love him, and he isn't always bad I guess. There are some moments where I enjoy talking to him, like when he's watching a show about animals, and I watch a little while passing by the living room. He tells me about the show, I talk back a little, and that's about all the socializing we do…At least I talked with him so he doesn't think I hate him.

I look at other people's parents and think, can they be my parents? Not saying my parents are horrible, I just wish they were more "normal", most likely my dad. I tend to get this feeling towards people who are old enough to be my dad. I would want other people's dad to be my dad, and it really would make me sad that they weren't my dad…weird, right? I think to myself, their child is going to be so loved and normal…not how I feel sometimes. I have to stop this weirdness. They have their own family. I should stop thinking about my potential life in theirs…but I don't think I could ever stop thinking like this. I love my dad; I just wish he could change a little (or a lot).

A dad shouldn't beat or yell at their children or wife. A dad should hug and kiss you, take care of you, go to your softball games, call you sweet names. I guess that's what I'm jealous of, that other people have those things and I don't. My dad takes care of me by paying for stuff, I guess. But just hugs and kisses me only when I leave for a long while (if that); anything more would be awkward at this point.

He makes me not trust him when he yells or hits me (go figure.) He says he loves me, but his actions and words are different. I would hear when my dad would yell and beat my mom; like he didn't even care I was in the house. Forgetting how I always feel, if he did feel, ignoring my screams for him to stop; I just want to feel truly loved and listened to.

****

"You need to make more friends."

"I can't make friends AND get good grades."

That's a lame excuse I guess, I just stress about my grades while trying to maintain my social life. I feel like I need good grades to have fun, I also get too depressed sometimes to talk to people…especially after I see my grades, and then start to compare. I only have one good friend here, that's good enough right? I made some on the retreat thing, but we don't really talk unless we pass each other on the way to classes. It's sad when people have to tell me to make friends.

"Talk to them about themselves, get a conversation going."

I try, but it never really works out.

"So where are you from?"

"Wisconsin."

"Do you like it there?"

"Yeah, it's okay."

And that's usually when the conversation ends and I don't know what else to say. Now whenever I'm in a conversation I get nervous, because I try to find "non-awkward" things to say. Sometimes I wonder why they would talk to me, nobody ever talks to me, but I don't wanna say, "Why are you talking to me?" They'll think I'm really weird then.

I only get really confident when I drink, which I shouldn't solely rely on. I'm only nineteen years old and I have been drinking since I was a freshman in high school. I just need that confidence sometimes, like when I go to a concert or a wedding; my parents would let me drink as long as I was around them…so they thought.

I guess it isn't totally okay what they do, but I think they teach me what my limitations are, and to never drink and drive. I drank and drove once, and it was really stupid, but I was lucky I didn't get caught or got in an accident. I wasn't blackout drunk or anything, like I could still walk a straight line, but still, not really a good excuse. I was at my friend's house, a group of us playing games and drinking. My "so called friend" got too drunk and our guy friend had to take us home. I thought it was a good idea I drive him back, everything was cloudy on the way back, and so was my drive back to her house alone. I was lucky nothing happened…so maybe I did drink a bit too much, oh well live and learn; it was a fun night, nonetheless (this was obviously before our little fight).

****

I need to learn to say things and be confident, and to not care so much about what others think of me (and to not rely on alcohol so much.) If I'm not good enough for them then forget them. I wonder sometimes how I turned out like this. The way I was raised wasn't like others. I had to put up with my dad yelling and beating my mom, but from all that, I turned out pretty okay I would say, I'm strong from the experiences I guess. I have good manners, treat people nicely, am respectful, the only thing that's wrong I guess is I have anxiety, over-think, and have depression, but it's not extreme like most cases. I learn to deal with it by not worrying so much, and finding things that make me happy, like coffee. Coffee makes me feel so great. I read an article not too long ago on Facebook saying something like, 'People who drink coffee are fifty-three percent less likely to commit suicide', probably because of all the caffeine. I guess I can agree with that statement, when I drink coffee, my whole mood changes and I feel like everything is good with my life.

Maybe yelling at your kids isn't so bad, it builds character. I sometimes feel like a baby for telling on my dad, because people back then didn't really care about abuse like they do now so why do people all of the sudden care? I guess people didn't take into consideration a lot of things back then, they were, and still are, just figuring things out. People didn't think cigarettes were bad back then, but then decided twenty years later they actually are bad. They didn't think drinking or guns were that bad, but they are. My point is I guess people care about abuse more now than they did back then. I decided it does affect people both physically and mentally…I guess I'm just old school, and think, it's okay to beat a person…that sounds really bad and not true.

I always felt bad for my dad, because he's depressed and has diabetes. I still do have fun with him and love him (when he's not yelling), and I know he loves us. Though he has a weird way of showing it; he likes having fun too, and I like seeing him have fun and not being depressed and yelling. My mom puts up with a lot. I know I have to be there for her. Also live my life and not worry about her all the time (which has been a struggle for me). Life's too short to be miserable all the time, there are great things and great people out there, and you just have to live your life.

* * *

Sometimes, I look at other people and think, "man who raised them"? They yell at their parents, rude to their friends, and disrespectful. They complain and don't seem grateful (guilty of some of this, but I'm not talking about me right now). Even at this age in college, what if your best friend stole your ex-boyfriend, you guys broke up. I never got that, what, the guy is 'off the market' because you dated him first? Okay. Maybe it's because I was never in that situation, but it just sounds bogus and stupid.' Your mom lets you stay out till what time? Doesn't she care?' When I had a fight with my "so-called friend", we were arguing, and she was pissed at me because my mom gave me a curfew, and now I guess we can't do anything together. She was saying my mom didn't care about me, so I said her mom doesn't care about her, letting her stay out till four A.M in Chicago, going out with strange guys. On our vacation, my friend told her mom that I think this way. Yes, you are a bad mom, and need to be firmer with your skanky little daughter…When my mom says be home at this time, I obey her. My so called friend's mom needs to set a curfew and not let her daughter run her life, she'll break it anyway, but she'll at least think she has boundaries.

She said she trusts her because she tells her the truth, which made me laugh inside. I should've told her about the weed she had, and the guy she sees, even though her mom told her not to see him. She probably wouldn't care, she'd just tell her mom she's depressed, and her mom would let her do whatever. If I say that to my mom, she won't let me out…I don't know, send her back to the mental facility if she keeps saying that. I sure would, geez, don't just say 'I give up' all the time. I heard her say that a thousand times- and that's just pathetic, saying I give up to your kid, and look at them now, they're all screwed now (I mean, so am I but still.) She really is a nice lady, but she just needs some parenting advice or something. It means nothing we're nineteen and adults now, and can technically do whatever. We still live under their roof, and should still respect them, and leaving my phone at the house when I'm really downtown so my mom doesn't see my location doesn't seem very respectful. Even older adults are rude. They probably learned it as kids. If someone is bugging you, either make up with them, nicely let them know they're bugging you, or walk away, don't be a child and fight them or keep yelling at them. I hope when I have kids I teach them to be respectful and have manners. Kids act the way they are mostly because of their parents, and maybe teachers; I learned the hard way.

"Come on, why you gotta chew like that, close your mouth!"

My dad would yell at the dinner table.

"Okay", I would say, trying not to cry…and that's how I learned to chew with my mouth closed.

I'm giving advice about being a parent even though I'm not one (apparently I shouldn't do that). Okay, do what makes you feel free and happy, just try not to die - live and learn. I give up! I really never know the right things to say anymore, 'do this, don't do this, wear this, and wear that'. I'm still probably gonna be figuring things out when I'm in my 30's.

****

There was this one time we were all eating dinner, my mom, dad, brother and me, and my dad was yelling at my mom and even hit her in front of us. I started to cry, because he was yelling, banged the table, and smacked my mom in front of me - I was about ten at the time.

"Why are you crying? I can't get angry? Fine, I'll sit over here and eat my dinner." He got up and went to the counter bar.

I feel bad now, I tried to stop crying but couldn't, my brother even glared at me to say 'shut up', My mom left the table at this point, so it was really awkward now. I could still see and hear his heavy sighs and his fork smacking the plate. I felt helpless, and a little stupid, because I made him leave the table. I of course felt bad for my mom, and felt like a baby for crying; I'm so precocious around him when he's mad. I'll gently close the door, I walk without making a sound, chew softly, watch TV at a low volume, try not to cough (he's yelled at me for that). I was in third grade.

"Get some medicine or something; I'm sick of hearing you cough!" He would yell.

I'm off to school now, sad and crying again! Heck, I don't even breathe that loud when I'm around him when he's mad. I just listen to his footsteps echo in the house, shaking everything in sight. I try to listen to music, but my headphones won't go loud enough. I would literally count how many nights in a row he would have his little moments, and got up to 2 weeks once when I was in freshman year of high school.

I hated hearing my dad eat, or do anything, when he's mad. He sighs loud all the time, slams his silver wear on his plate, chomps his food, and just looks like he's gonna kill somebody. So yeah, that's how I got my manners, by people yelling at me that I'm doing something wrong (also why I hate loud noises). Again, maybe this abuse isn't so bad, you might have some mental scars, but you eventually grow from them.

6

CONFUSION

I am a child of God, that's what I am, but other than that? I am a girl, for starters, and the rest is all a bit unclear. I guess I'm an athlete, even though I feel like I'm not sometimes, because I suck at pretty much every sport, and complain when I have to practice, a true athlete doesn't do that. I play the trumpet, what an eye-catcher right? Being in the band right, pretty much screams loser, according to some people, but I like playing the trumpet (better than softball,) and at least I get to play. I honestly don't know what else I'm "actually" good at (besides complaining). I'm good at being me, awkward, nice, funny, me. I learned you never really get rid of your awkwardness; you just have to embrace it. I don't even think I'm that awkward. I just let out a tiny little scream when I run into people, then walk away. You may grow out of your awkwardness, but it will always come back a little, and be a part of you. I am who I am because I'm awkward, and some people like that. My friends in high school were awkward, and I think they are awesome, and made me not feel as bad about being awkward, hey, at least I made friends.

Maybe what made me so awkward was because I met them, and because my mom kept telling me my friends are awkward. I don't really know why she said they were awkward, probably because they liked me, and they were in band class also. We made fun of the 'Blonde Squad' at school, they were all blonde, obviously, and hung around the stupid boys, acting like them, and being annoying like them. They would always be hanging out together, and making stupid noises in class, and laughing at stupid things. We would always complain about having them in one of our classes.

"I got annoying people in my class, Mitch, Jake, Blake, and the 'Blonde Squad'."

It's not like we hated them. They were just a little annoying, and we like complaining about them and how they act all peppy and slutty, we weren't being totally mean though, so it wasn't really bullying. I didn't really like them because they made no effort to be my friend. Maybe I could've made an effort, but I don't want to come off desperate for friends. But I guess that's how you make friends. The majority of the 'Blonde Squad' was in softball with me. They were the ones who didn't really listen to me or not really acknowledge me, which made me think of them as peppy jerks. They all obviously played more than me too. I think that's because they went to the partner grade school that works with the high school, and the coach favors certain people, obviously not me, I never expected much anyway.

I might've been a little jealous of them because they looked and acted more "normal" than me. They were more social, having nice hair, being more athletic, having "normal" dads (and they do, because I met them, and they go to events and talk to people, unlike mine). I would cry, thinking how "normal" other people's lives are then mine. I bet their mom doesn't complain that her life is so miserable. I bet their dad acknowledges them and shows his love. I bet their dad doesn't scream, hit, or call their wife and children names. I bet they don't think about why I'm so shy, and seem sad all the time, no one likes talking about that stuff, right?

I try not to think about how abnormal my life is, because it just makes me sad. I try to think about how I overcame things; visions of my dad dragging my mom across the floor, and her screaming, run through my mind, I can't control it. I just need to talk to people about it, and have fun right now. It just sucks how people don't understand. I can't just blurt it out in a conversation, 'hey my dad hits my mom sometimes'; you should get to know someone before you try to explain your life to them, if even then.

****

I was in cheerleading my freshman year of high school, and never went back, for multiple reasons. We were on our way to cheer camp, when a member of the soon to be 'Blonde Squad' sat next to me. She chose ME! She showed me her tumbling videos and gave me her Snapchat. We then, a while later, stopped at McDonalds for breakfast, and then on the way back, she sat next to this other girl. When she got back on the bus, she did the same thing, showing her awesome tumbling videos. I was then alone, just listening to my music. Maybe I didn't make enough of an effort to talk back to her...She probably left because I'm awkward and she didn't want it to rub off on her. Being alone in my bus seat I thought, 'man I wish I could tumble like her, maybe we can be friends, and she can teach me?' When we got to our destination, everyone was amazed she could cheer, tumble, and fly so well, so she made friends real quick, meanwhile, all I wanted to do was go home.

I liked cheer, but I wasn't good enough, the coaches were annoying, and I didn't even cheer in the tournaments I was so bad. I knew there would never be hope, so I quit and went to pep band and bowling (more my speed.) Was I good at those things? Not really…but I had a ball (literally).

I really loved band class; my weird but awesome friends were in band, the tours were fun, I loved playing the trumpet, the band director was awesome and fun, it was all over great. I knew 100% I would do band in college, so I auditioned for a scholarship for band at this college I wanted to go to. I thought I did well, until I didn't get the scholarship, whelp, guess I really didn't do so well…can cross that college off my list. I wanted to audition at the college I'm at now, but they gave away all their scholarships, I probably wouldn't have made it anyway. I was already committed to do softball anyway according to my mom, and I did.

I formed a bowling club in college, like I actually formed it. I dealt with the finances and everything…not many people go, but I'm hoping next year I'll advertise more and get more people to join. I love bowling, even though I'm bad at it.

I'm in softball now, and if I could go back, I'd probably do band instead. I hear they only have two trumpets, figures, and if I join next year they'll probably have like 10. The reason I say 'probably do band' is because, I kind of like softball now (even though I don't play much). It's cool being in a college sport. It's true, I guess; sports are good for your mental health. Sure, I get depressed and don't want to go to practices and games half the time. And I'm failing psychology…but when I get there, It's actually not so bad, and I'm not that bad, I'm decent. I think it's because your brain focuses on the sport you're playing, so you don't think about the depressing thoughts you have…I get back to my old sad self, eventually.

I do miss band though, and there are some pretty cool people in the band. I've talked to people in the band. They say hi to me in the hallway, and sit with me at lunch. They sense it, no softball people do that, don't get me wrong, they're nice people, I'm just proving a point that some pretty cool people are in band, well my definition of cool people anyway. Great, now I wanna do band.

I think about next year too much. This college class I'm taking wants me to map out my next three years. Like I don't know, that's too far ahead for me, they tell you not to worry about the future, and give us this? I'm so confused…I guess it's true, college doesn't just play around.

****

I think I gave up discovering who I am. I'm just me, which I apparently can't explain…explaining why I stood up in front of class for about ten seconds not saying anything when I gave my speech about myself. The speech had to be about me, and it's hard when you don't know who you are exactly. I said I was like a book, you have to read me to really know me, if I was in the audience listening to me, I wouldn't read that book. I knew where I was going with that pitch, I just didn't say all the right things…shocker.

I try to find the things I'm good at, sports? School…? Music…? Acting…? Singing…? Art…? Dancing…? Comedy…? Scuba Diving…? I don't know, I try things but they never seem to work out as I had hoped. I tried almost every sport in high school. The only sport I was decent at was softball. The only sport I've been decent at and been playing since I was five, is softball. Out of the three other sports I did, I'm good at one, one out of four, that's twenty five percent of sports I'm good at. I don't care anymore, as long as I have fun and try my best, so I'm not good at things, most people aren't anyway, I'll just be a band geek, which I'm fine with, actually.

My coach told me to get into travel softball (great more money). I never knew of travel softball until freshman year of high school. When he told me, and other people who actually play in the games have been in travel ball since they were ten, which is apparently the top thing, and how you get playing time.

"They won't play you in games unless you're in travel softball". The assistant coach in softball told me.

Okay, I want to play, so I signed up for travel ball, which is way more expensive than just plain district softball, like, a thousand dollar difference, they don't mess around. I thought who would spend that much just to play softball? I swear that's all there is now, everything is so competitive now, literally everything is so competitive, and I don't think I like it honestly.

This (midget) girl in my grade got to play when she was only a freshman on the varsity team. Granted, we only had one team and it was small. But it was still a combination of varsity and JV, so we were all technically on varsity, but we did have some JV games in the season, meaning junior varsity. The reason I was so jealous of her was because everyone worshiped her, she wasn't that good, and the little girl bullied me in grade school…The bullies get everything. We were friends in high school, I was jealous because of the whole stupid softball thing…she wasn't even on a travel team, so that whole speech I got from my coach was a giant joke! Whatever, travel softball was fun I guess.

I can't really explain or give a good reason why I don't like her, I just don't, she's just that person you don't like for no valid reason. She's good at everything, smart, everyone likes her, and her family is perfect, or to me they seemed almost perfect. She can do no wrong. Like that game I told you about when we collided into each other. It was an error on both our parts but he took me out instead of her. She had the nerve to say it's my fault. I wanted to smack her. IT WAS BOTH OUR FAULT…apparently she did call it (which I didn't hear), I was about to call it before I hit her big head. When she's on base and makes an error, the coach gently says what she should do right, if I make an error, he screams at me. I didn't like him that much, is all I could say. He's a great person, just an unfair coach, but what coach is fair? All they care about is winning. The games turn out to be stressful and no fun, because the coaches yell all the time, and laugh about it later…so I guess it's like my life. I did like my tennis and bowling coach. I liked those sports better, they were laid back and fun to be around, I could make a mistake, and they wouldn't yell at me. People who yell at me rarely deserve my respect…How are you gonna yell at a person because they made a mistake or lost the game? Sports have probably ruined so many lives.

So yeah, everyone loved her and not me, at least that's how I felt. I would come to practice wanting to go home, even if it was hell at home, I wanted to go to my mom or hang with my friends. That's when high school ruined softball for me. I pretty much gave up at this point, well kind of, I would just be me, and go with the flow, it's not like they'll play me if I do good at practice. At practice, I caught about every ball that came to me, but I never played, he would never give me a chance. It's fine though, totally fine. I'm playing in college now, and if it goes south I'm switching to band. Coaches always play their favorites, and I'm never one of them.

****

Since I don't think I have a great a chance at getting a good job or doing great in school, I decided to write a book. Let's see how this goes.

"My life sucks…The end."

I like short and sweet, but I think that's a little too short. What really am I thinking…? I can't write a book, well I can but it probably won't be any good. Most people complain their life sucks, or that it's not how it turned out. I hear so many people say, 'I can't wait to die' or, 'I'm gonna jump off a cliff'. I heard my roommate the other day say, 'I was gonna go to this school because it is by the lake, so when I get stressed I can jump in and die'. I was thinking, 'oh you, too?', but I just laughed and said me too, so I can write about that, I guess. I should probably focus more on school than trying to be a writer anyway. People say that shit only when they're stressed, anyway. They don't when everything is going okay. I'm guilty of this. Things can be going not the way I want them, and I'll get really pissed. I say I want to die, but I'm learning to not say that as much. I don't really want to die, I just want the world to end…my dad made me like this, good excuse, blame your parent (s).

I honestly feel like I should be more stressed than I am right now, it's just the college thing to do. I'm not stressed when it comes to tests or exams, just when I get the grade back and find out I failed. I stress about my social life more than anything, like what to say when I'm around people, getting the urge to say hello, will they like me or not? I will think of things in my head to say to them, but then not say them, because I think they sound stupid and I'm scared to say them out loud.

I just give up on everything. I try to make friends. It doesn't work. I try to do well on tests, it doesn't work. I ask this girl to invite me to parties, she doesn't. I see her on Snapchat every weekend at a party, like thanks for telling me, like I asked you to… she must not want me there, I'll cramp her style, that's fine. Whatever, I need to focus on school anyway. I'm just gonna do things that make me happy: drink, smoke, play around, anything…or just cry, which actually makes me feel a bit better.

I'm thinking of transferring and it's not even been 5 months yet. What will transferring really do? What if I don't like that school? I can't keep transferring back and forth to schools. I think about dropping out a lot, but then I'll be a college dropout, and I don't want that. What will I do then, what good jobs can I get? What even is a degree? People start their own business and don't have a degree. That's what I'll do, start my own business…I think about dropping out during softball practice, during school, after school, my head hurts from thinking about this so much. I'll just be sitting in class, staring at the board, thinking about my future, and not about class (probably why I do badly in class).

Is this even worth it? Paying all this freaking money to go to college and learn things I don't even need for my major that I don't even know yet? Yes, it is, if I want a good paying job it is. But I don't even know what I want my major to be? A Lawyer…? A teacher…? A physical therapist…? An engineer…? There are so many options. They all take too much time; I don't want to be in school for eight years…I'm convinced, and hoping the world will end before I graduate college. I came up with the idea of majoring in environmental science, because I like being outdoors. But the major requires too much chemistry, and I suck at chemistry. Now, I'm thinking of exercise science, it involves chemistry, but not as much, but do I see myself doing that for the rest of my life? I don't know…plus I'm bad at biology and wanted to cry the whole time, but that's college right.

I'm currently having a mental breakdown that lasted about half the year now; thoughts about softball, college is stupid, the trip we're going on, how I'm failing two classes. I just need to study more and get my grades up…I miss back home, some guy stole a hundred dollars from me, I'm thinking of dropping out, thoughts of suicide, trying to balance all this. Please God help me!

I bet this is God's way of punishing me, wanting to experiment with guys. When I had him over, the bastard stole my hundred out of my wallet. I know it was him, he asked me for a forty the other day because he got kicked out of his dad's house. I felt bad. So I stupidly gave it to him, even though I barely knew him. He used me, he seemed so nice, but it was obviously just a mask. I was so mad, I'm never going to get over this, or trust guys, and I'm also deleting Tinder. So this is what I get for trying.

****

I ponder everything I learn in class.

"Electrons get transported through the electron transport chain, to create ATP".

Okay, but instead of knowing all the steps, can't I just know that mitochondria is where cellular respiration happens, why do I need to know all the steps on how it works? It's useless History.

"Baldwin the first died so his son Baldwin the second took over, then his son Baldwin the third took over, then his son, Pons, took over".

Um…okay? I study and study, and still manage to fail. All I need to know about history is how countries were discovered, and some battles. I don't care about all the names, and they're honestly useless. When am I ever gonna talk about this again? I guess it could be a good conversation starter…and I thought we should forget the past anyway? Why should I learn this if I'm never going to use this again anyway?

Oh yeah and guess what? They're raising tuition next year, and apparently they do that every year, by about $995. I thought we are supposed to be making college affordable? I have to get a good job now to pay all this money back, and need to really make college worth it now. People say it's not all about the money, but it kind of is nowadays. I try not to think about the money and just rely on God. But I want to be able to afford a house, and things that I want, and I need a good paying job for that, or do I? I guess people make a living off just working at McDonalds, right? So I should be fine. I'll choose a major that makes me happy, now what is that exactly?

I'm so lost; I don't know if I'll be back, I don't know my major, I don't know if I'll be on softball next year, I don't know anything. But that's okay, right?

7

HOME

Not this place, nope, this is NOT and will never be home…I'm talking about college. I had to write a paper for my college class. He asked me to write about if 'college is home or not' maybe for some people it is, but it is not home for me. Home is where the heart is, where the people you love the most are, where you feel the most comfortable at. College is like a glorified prison, I feel trapped, it's kind of comfortable, and I have some fun…but still not home. My heart isn't at college, my heart is at home with my family, hence why I think about home all the time. I have some people I like here, but they're not my family. I wish some people where, like that guy I talk to, what if he was my dad instead of my real dad? It's weird and wrong to think of that, plus it's not what God intended, but is it really wrong, wishing to have someone else's life, what if they think the same thing? I don't think of it that way, I think of it as just imagining him as my dad, like a father figure, which is kind of the same thing, right? It does seem strange, but I bet I'm not the only one who thinks like this…that's fine.

It's probably not a good thing to do, because I start liking the other person more than my real dad, and want him as my dad. I feel weird saying this, but I compare the two. I obviously go towards the other person, because they probably don't yell around their kids and beat their wife, and their kids are probably not screwed up like me. Again, I can't really control my thoughts. I love my dad. I really do (though it may not seem like it,) I just think a lot and have an active imagination…that's probably slowly destroying me…but, it's fine.

You probably think I hate my dad with a passion, I don't hate him, I love him, I just don't love him at certain times, like when he yells and hits people. I just need to love and live my life right now, which I'm in the process of doing. I need to realize that this is my crazy life. My dad gets in a wild mood and hits and yells, and then forgets about it in the morning. My mom will be crying that night, and act fine the next morning…I guess if you can't beat 'em join 'em; I need to forget the past.

I haven't been home in so long I forgot what it feels like; right now I'm focusing on not failing out of college, which isn't going so well. Part of me says college is stupid and pointless, the other part says 'it'll get you a good job, just stick it out,' but will it? I feel like there are a lot of decent jobs out there you don't need college for, I don't know of any right now, but I'm sure there are some. The thing I don't understand is you have to go to college now to be what my dad is. He didn't go to college back then, and he's just as successful…times change so much, and I can't really do anything about it, besides complain.

What will I do if I drop out, anyway? I'll be home then, and have to get any job I can get. I would probably end up going to a community college; I don't want to do anything at this point, I want the world to end, but I obviously can't control that. College is making me a more miserable person than I already am. I study my ass off but I still fail, that's college I guess; college is meant for smart people, so what am I doing here? I need to talk to someone that'll listen to me complain, but I feel bad doing that, and what advice can they give me that I know I won't listen to anyway? I am a complex person, I can literally be happy one minute, but that can change in a split second. I just don't want to fail at life, which I'm kind of doing right now.

The part I really miss about home is my dog Spencer, my little golden doodle that people say takes after me because we're both slow and stupid. I just want to pick him up and hug him, he looks like a white fluffy baby bear, and every time I think of him I smile.

I feel like the more I say 'I want to go home', God's going to bring me home, like to Heaven. That's why I say I want to go home as back in Illinois where my family is. That sounds better, because I don't want to go to Heaven yet…that's not up to me either I know.

I've been thinking about killing myself again…but I'm pretty sure I won't do that. I'm just so stressed, and that would be the easy way out; I know nobody wants me to kill myself, things are bad, but they're are never that bad, there's always something good, like: God, coffee, that guy I talk to (which I probably annoy), my best friend I found, participating in events like archery club. It changes my whole mood, I swear. This is what makes me happy; I guess I'm kind of getting to like college.

I want to give up most times…but this is college, the big leagues. I can't just give up, I mean I can, but it's a battle of what I should and should not do, and I should not give up. I just hate failing in everything. Even though I freaking studying, I forget the material by the time the test comes. I'll think I filled out the right answer on the test, but then I get it back and realize it was the wrong answer. Or the answer I thought was right, was the only one I got right…Maybe I don't study enough, honestly I don't know what's enough anymore, all I know is that I need a change.

As soon as I got back from spring break, I was in a good mood, I thought it would last, but it eventually wore off. If only I wasn't failing these classes. If only I was home. If only my life was different, if only I had someone to talk to, but none of that compares with what God says, if only I can hear Him. You even need to go to college to 'professionally talk to people' as in a therapist. And that sometimes doesn't fully help, maybe I should just rely on God fully, it's honestly less stressful when I do that, that's what I'll do, what classes will I take next year? I don't know; that's up to God to decide, if only it worked that way, but does it? I. Don't. Know. All

I know is I love and trust God, thanking Him everyday, and hoping things will work out.

8

HELP

Knock-knock…? Who's there? No one…Thanks for the help. Whenever I seek help, I can't seem to find any. Well, I might find some help, and it obviously helps in the moment, but some things don't really help. You can give me 20 pieces of advice, and I will most likely forget all of them… remembering maybe one bit of advice.

I don't know how much others can really help me, and I can usually guess their answers before they say them. Why shouldn't I kill myself? Because you don't want to go to Hell and people WILL miss you. I'm failing a class. What should I do? Study...I just need to deal with my problems on my own, and I never know what to say when I go to people? I guess it just helps talking to people. I sometimes say 'I don't know what to say', and they help me out by saying things I should say. I'm learning to be more forward with people and telling them how I'm really feeling inside. It's actually been really helpful, because others have some pretty good advice, and it feels better getting things off my chest. It seems like they know more than me…I guess that's why they get paid.

"So why are you here?"

"I don't know, I'm just stressed and need to talk to someone."

Then the conversation starts off and the other person might say something like 'why are you so stressed', then I will explain why I am. I don't know how people can help me when I can't help myself, I guess it's because they're smarter than me and they got a degree to "professionally talk to people". When I say that stuff to my friends, they usually just say me, too. Except my friend from college, she actually helps me. That's why I like her so much. She'll actually give me some helpful advice, or we'll take a walk somewhere to ease our minds, talking about our classes we're in, laughing about what some person said in class.

I really wish you could take a mental health day off for college, but I feel bad skipping class, I did one time and felt bad afterwards. I just didn't feel like going to Taekwondo, and didn't feel like kicking things; it felt good to sleep all day. I want to skip this biology lab because it's freaking long and pointless. But I'll definitely fail if I skip…like why do I need to make bacteria grow, aren't we supposed to be preventing that? 'Make sure to wear gloves because this stuff can make you really sick if it gets on you'; okay, I'm going to sue the school if I die from this lab.

Most of these classes are bullshit, but I have to take them anyway. Please tell me why I have to take history for my major, since when do you need it for exercise science? Whatever I do, I know I won't need history for it. I could just drop the class, but I need to take one eventually to graduate…but I'm failing…ugh.

Can't I call in sick, like what people do for work? I did that for high school, but this is college, and you could miss a whole lot more, plus, I have to go to class to learn to dissect a pig and grow bacteria.

****

Parents are there to help you right? Well they're supposed to anyway.

"Mom, doing school and softball is so stressful I can't concentrate and I hate everything…I want to drop out."

"Well then quit and work at Dunkin Donuts all your life!"

Is that helping? Is it tough love? I don't know, it makes me more confused though is all I know…and I do like coffee. It's not like I hate softball, I like it…I don't know if I want to quit or not, I'll play this year out I guess. I'm leaning towards quitting, and joining band, but I don't know for sure. I'll probably know the week before I have to start sophomore year. I just don't want to disappoint my mom.

Does everybody have a college adviser, if so, do they help? I feel like my adviser doesn't help as much. I gave him my tentative schedule for next year, and he just glanced at it and approved it. But I don't think he took time to really read it; I sent the schedule to my mom.

"You can't take two psychology classes, and don't take an anthropology class. What do you need that for? You need to talk to someone else who will help you more."

I really want to drop out at this point. I already had a mental breakdown in biology…failure. And 'why' questions came in my mind and all I wanted to do was cry and storm out of the room, I was just staring blankly with my head down looking sad.

'Why do I have to take these classes if it doesn't relate to my major? Why can't I concentrate? Why do I have to learn this? When will I use this in life? I probably won't even be successful. This is stupid. I hate college.'

Tears then started to build up, but I just tried starting to think positively.

'Only a month left, summer is coming, freedom, relaxation, you will get through this and be successful!' Wow, that really does help…only for so long though, before the negative thoughts come back.

I think my stupidity started when I failed an open note test, people were like 'how do you do that'? It's really not hard to understand, you just take bad notes, and therefore you have no-good notes for the test.

That pill bottle never looked so good, but I can't do that to my family and friends. Plus the fact I'll probably go to Hell. Maybe, no one, not even pastors know for sure where you go. I asked.

I just find hope in the future: summer, hanging out with friends and my mom, sleeping in, coffee, no school, no homework, and no stress. I just hope my dad won't be in his moods all summer; is it weird that I expect them? I do hate when he gets like that, but it gives me something to complain about, and it makes me not regret calling DCFS when I was a junior in high school. The only reason I regret calling is because it didn't really do anything, and he didn't hit me hard, so that's why I feel bad. He was apparently in a good mood when the cops came…that didn't last long. He's really good at acting like the Devil one moment, then acting like he had an exorcism the next day, and is a whole new person.

Everyone says that's a poor excuse and I shouldn't regret calling, but I do sometimes, and even my mom does sometimes too.

I don't really know what I wanted to accomplish when I did it, I was just so pissed off and wanted things to change, but it didn't really help. My therapist at school told me I could call them if I wanted to, so I'm like what the heck.

She said they would show up at school, if I decide to call them. I guess the only reason I called them was because they would show up at school first and not at my house, to see if it was a "real" problem or not. Guess what? They showed up at my house.

I got a call from my mom yelling and screaming at me, saying she was outside waiting for me. I got in the car, and she told me the cops and DCFS were coming to the house and I can't stay there anymore. Well, at least I'll have to get out for two weeks, so I stayed at my grandma's house for about two weeks, and was depressed about everyday…Did I do the right thing? She said I did, but I really don't know anymore. When the two weeks were up, I went back home. We obviously went on like nothing ever happened, people say I should just talk to my dad about how I feel, but he's not the easiest to talk to…plus he scares me a little.

"You two need to talk more and hug, let him know you love him."

"Okay."

Well, I do love him; it's just a little awkward considering I tried to get him arrested. I honestly don't think we'll ever have a normal relationship. I'm pretty sure he still knows I love him.

When I came back home, we still didn't talk much. I was just done trying to fix things and try to live a more "normal" life, my life will never be "normal" and I'm just gonna have to live with that.

****

Back to college, I'm down to 2 weeks left in freshman year. My softball team is planning to have a softball game in dedication to the girl who passed away on our team. We ended up playing each other because the other team bailed on us. Yes, I get to play. If I do well I can maybe travel with the "varsity" team to the next game and actually play! I was up to bat; I fouled the ball two times; okay, one more, the ball passes, and strike three.

"Shit!" I mumbled loudly under my breath and walked in the dugout, acting like I wasn't as pissed off as I seemed to be. Thoughts of course came to my mind.

'Why do I suck at everything I do? I blew my only chance to play in a varsity game. He'll never give me another chance. I'm definitely quitting next year, so what now I'm a quitter? What does that say about me? I have no friends on the team, they probably wouldn't even ask about me next year. I bet the girl who died would've been better than me, it should've been me. I hate everything, I want a second chance, but who believes in those anymore?'

I was two girls away from being up again in the seventh inning, but this fast short girl stole every base and we won, so I didn't get a chance to bat. Great, another 'good at everything' midget on the team…I acted like I was happy, but I wanted to cry, such a baby right, I didn't get what I wanted so I want to cry. It's a situation I expect no one to understand because nobody understands me and my thoughts. I could've thrown a big fit about not batting again, but

I just played it cool, it's not the end of the world, I'm just upset I didn't get to recover myself.

I told God in my mind that if I didn't bat again, I'd go back to my dorm and cut myself. Wow. He wants me to cut myself, He's okay with that? I'm positive He doesn't want me to do that, I'm just being a brat, as my mom would say. I went back and put the scissors to my wrist, and sliced it down my wrist, enough to leave a scar, but not draw blood…I guess that's good. What does this prove…that I'm depressed? It doesn't take away what happened, but it somehow helps me, though I know it's stupid and wrong.

I have visions of me crying hysterically and cutting my wrists up, but in reality, I know cutting is wrong, and I only make two or three cuts, while thinking how stupid this is. I know no one wants me to cut, so during the whole process that's what I'm thinking of, and what do the scars mean; that I'm depressed and want people to know that? It's kind of yes and kind of no. When most people look at scars on wrists they think of two things; 'she's messed up I don't want to be around her', or, 'I want to ask her what's wrong and help her. I don't want either of those things.

I watched a video on YouTube the other day of this girl who killed herself because nobody would listen. She took pills and died. Her mom found her dead on the carpet with foam in her mouth. The dad came in and tried CPR on her but nothing worked, the mom, her sisters, and the dad were all hysterical, this even made me cry, their lives were changed forever for the worst. I watched the video to see what overdosing was like, and it makes you really sick. It at least made me not want to do it. All the people it affected…I guess it's good I watched the video.

It got me thinking I would never want to put my family through any of that, finding your own daughter or sibling dead on the floor? Just thinking of it makes me cry. I pray nobody has to go through that, and I'm glad it scared me straight.

I found this other video, completely random, as I was sad and listening to music on YouTube. I scrolled by this video titled, "Please Don't kill yourself". It was rap by this guy, Clayton Jennings, it wasn't a song, but like a poem of him talking about not killing yourself. There are these three people with a switchblade, pills, and a gun, all ready to kill themselves. They put those things away, as this guy raps to them, about not killing yourself, and how people love you. I was bawling my eyes out on my bed, watching the video.

The video talks about how God wants to help you through this mess, and the devil puts these thoughts of suicide in your mind, not God. Days might've sucked back then, but you can change them in the future, one day is worse than the next, the next might be better, live for your family, friends, and yourself. Some might say 'well no one cares about me'. There is always someone out there who cares: a pastor, a parent, a sibling, a neighbor, and the police. Trust me; no one wants you to kill yourself, even if a person doesn't know you, theirs, and my heart breaks every time I here about someone taking their own life.

I cry every time I watch the video, because it's such a powerful message. It makes me think of whom I will hurt if I kill myself, and the video brings me closer to God, in asking for help, and knowing how much He loves me. The Devil and God are both powerful people. The devil wants nothing but to destroy things, so he puts those thoughts in your mind hoping you'll do it. But God wants to save you from those thoughts and bring you comfort, I know it sometimes doesn't seem like God is there, but He always is. Think of better days ahead. Those videos I mentioned help get those thoughts away fast. Even thinking about it, people who think about it those things, need to go talk to people. Even if you are not going to do it but still think about it, go talk, it really helps to just let your feelings and thoughts out. God definitely sent this video to me.

9

FACTS

I always look forward to summer, even though I'm bored a majority of the time. I get to be home with my mom, take a break from school, catch up on sleep, catch up on TV, hang out with friends more, what more could I ask for? Well, I wouldn't mind going on vacations to different places I see everyone going to, even if it's just out of state to Wisconsin or something, I'd be happy with that. Well, I did go on vacation with my "so-called friend" this summer and last summer, and that didn't go as planned. I got another upcoming vacation with another friend of mine, but they're kind of…different. I say different just because they're just the opposite of my family, and they annoy me more…which is saying a lot. Her mom, for one, gets stressed while driving. Even with a GPS, she'll get lost, and yell in the tiny car. I play music and put my headphones in, but I could still hear her yell, and it's worse than my dad, my ears actually ring. So now I'm stressed and having mental breakdowns. I'm homesick, and just want to go home. I try to make the best of it though, it's not all bad, they're nice people nonetheless, and I do have fun. I just obviously don't like yelling.

But yeah…you ever want to go home so bad but can't? It sucks, you desperately want to go home, and that's all you think about, then you get depressed and think about all the things wrong with your life…well at least I do. Why did I get myself into this again? Why am I not like other girls my age? Am I being selfish? I hate this vacation. I actually goggled bus routes to get home; I wanted to leave so badly. We're just sitting in the motel room watching

TV…something I would be doing if I was home, in my own tiny comfy bedroom.

I say again 'why did I get myself into this AGAIN'? Because I went twice already in the past years and was just as stressed on all of them. The majority of the time there's yelling and doing nothing, just wanting to go home, and hiding my tears. It doesn't seem much of a vacation. And what they say to each other, the attitude and shouting the mom and daughter use to the dad. My mom would smack me to oblivion, if I spoke like that. They honestly call him stupid and yell at him most of the time. And he's an IT so he's not stupid at all. He needs to step up and stand his ground, if you ask me. Tell them how to respect others, discipline them, and yes, the mother too, tell them to shut the hell up and stop yelling; you already know what my dad would do.

It's awkward, too, because I'm the guest on the vacation. I don't want to say anything to make them hate me. I just sit in the back with my headphones on. Still listening to them yelling and text complaining to my mom and friends, and not to mention it's extremely rude what they do, yelling in front of their guest. But who am I to judge? I honestly don't know how someone can get that stressed and yell so much. And over stupid little things that can be solved without yelling. Nothing is ever that bad you have to yell that loud. Things may get stressful and not go as planned, but you just have to calmly deal with it. You'll go nowhere in life freaking out over things…but yeah, I'm used to this, living with my dad and all.

It is pretty amusing listening to them argue. I'll have to say that. But mostly annoying; I honestly don't know how they stay together, but then again, I don't know how my parents have stayed together this long, either? What with them being on their tenth divorce they threaten they are going to get…maybe arguing is good for a relationship? My friend yells at her mom to tell her to stop yelling, but that doesn't help much (shocker). It just creates more yelling. And the dad just sits there like it's normal. Like do something! Be a demanding father and husband; they both need to calm down and hide their anxiety and yelling, like other people do, I have tried to calm my friend down but it doesn't really help.

"You need to calm down, don't yell, it's not that bad."

"I'm not yelling, I'm just annoyed, just leave me alone!"

Okay, I tried, whatever, that's fine, only 5 more days…I only went the two other times, because I felt bad for my friend because she doesn't have many other friends. She's an only child. Also I have no excuse not to go. And I don't want them to think I don't want to go because they yell too much, even though that's the case. I did try one time to make an excuse not to go…and they moved the date so I could go, again, whatever I tried, it's only two weeks. I don't even know why she likes me going, I'm boring and don't talk much, I'm sure her other friends will be more than fun. You think being the strong Christian family they are, they won't be like that, but you'd be wrong. I guess I should be honored she likes me so much, and I like her she's my friend…just two weeks is a lot.

My friend has even complained to me how she hates when her mom and dad argue, which makes me feel worse if I don't go with them, because she is still my friend. So that's how I keep going, even though I say I'm not going with them again. She's really different from my other friends. She makes weird noises, yells too much, and talks way more than necessary. Like when she tells a story she tells, the, whole, story, like word for word what the person said, and her mimicking voice, ugh, don't get me started. I'm so sick of people yelling and not acting their age, like act your age and be an adult, stop whining over spilled milk; you will go nowhere, acting like this. I just want a normal vacation with no extreme yelling, but what is normal anyway.

I honestly have anxiety 24/7 when I'm with them, because they take forever to do things. They yell the majority of the time, and eat at abnormal times, so I'm starving until they want to eat. There was one time I didn't even care and was gonna starve myself till the end of the trip. You have to have been there to see it really. Maybe it's just because we're so different. It's my own fault for going I guess. I just have a big ass heart and can't say no, I just try to accept their differences, and realize God made them the way they are, weirdness and all. You think I'd learn by now and not go, but I can't say no…and not even my excuses work. Screw it though; I need to start doing what I want to do. To think all this started because I jokingly said I'd go to California with you…and she took it not as a joke, so here I am.

I prefer vacations with my family, like the skiing trip we take every year, we go up to this cool cabin in Wisconsin. I love it up there (and to just get away). Everyone is super nice. It's in the country, you can see the stars. I sort of love skiing. The cabin is awesome and cozy, no, or minimum yelling and, we drink, I just love it there. I'm rarely stressed at all, and just deal with my dads yelling by this point and accept it.

I guess I also said yes to vacation with her and her family, because I get out, and it's something to do. But anyway that's all the vacation I go on, TWO a year…how fun. I guess that's more than most people. I think I've seen enough marriages and people acting the wrong way that I know how to act the right way, and make my marriage go the right way…if I ever get married.

I learned a little about their past while I'm with them, and understand why they're screwed up. I guess they have a history of bipolar in the family, but she isn't bipolar, so why does she act this way? Maybe she needs some medication or something, I don't know. But she needs to learn to deal with her stress without yelling, that's all I know…actually, I think she has ADHD, which explains why she talks so much. It's all about how you deal with your stress and anxiety, and you have to learn to control it calmly, which is hard.

Summer is also a time where I think a lot. I think about what the future will hold. What job I will have? What guy I will marry? Will my parents ever get divorced? If going back to college is worth it? Will I make more friends at college, and will my depression worsen? I think about all those things and more. When I do nothing, I think about what my "so-called friend" said, I do nothing and have no friends. At least I have real friends. I bet she's jealous, because she has to work and pay for things already. While my mom is generous enough to help me with things…she probably said that shit out of anger too. Despite everything, I love her so much, and I hope we recover from our little fight…I am actually super grateful for her, and our crazy adventures we had. I'm confident we'll be fine, we're family, practically.

Summer is so relaxing, but it really does get old and actually makes me miss school a little. At least it makes me miss school, and makes me wanna go back. Probably not so much to others who vacation all summer long and have 'great' summers…maybe me missing school will give me motivation to do good? I get depressed during summer because I'm so bored, and I kind of don't like my life most of the time, so I'll settle for my second home. If I can just shake this depression thing off I'd be fine, if only it was that easy right. When my dad yells, is when my depression really kicks in. I can't sleep, yet I'm tired. I can't eat. I get anxiety. The sound of him yelling and swearing makes me sick to my stomach. I don't know what to do, besides ignore him, and talk my mom into divorcing him, which I don't know if I really want that, or if she'll ever do it.

We talk time and time about her divorcing my dad, we'd be in the car.

"So would you ever divorce dad?"

"Maybe, it's getting easier and easier to leave him."

Wow, only took you thirty years to realize that, but it never happened and probably never will, even though I sometimes pray for the day. I do feel bad for him, and don't really want a divorce, but I too am getting sicker and sicker of this shit he puts on us. If only leaving was that easy.

I mostly love when I'm with my mom, family, and friends, I only love my dad when he's not yelling, and even then he annoys me sometimes. I'm the type of person who will and has blown my friends off to hang with my mom. She's the only person who understands me more; because she goes through most of the things I go through. I want to spend time with her, because she does so much for me, and I love her. She's more fun sometimes anyway.

I honestly don't know where I'd be without her. I would tell myself I would kill myself if she were to die before me. But I realize it's selfish to think like that, and I put others in prospective that would miss me. It should never be that bad that I have to kill myself, over what, that I want a new life? That does seem selfish, it's like telling God He messed up, but really we mess up.

It may seem unfair, but God has a plan, and he plans for me and a bunch of others to be with Him in the end. We just have to get through this part first before we can get to paradise. I always think of the verse that says we may not know what God's doing with our life, but we soon will, it goes something along those lines. Whenever shit happens in my life, like when I had to call the cops on my dad, I just trusted God's plan. I trust I will learn from this, and all I learned from that is my dad is an ass, but it did change things, he doesn't beat my mom so hard anymore. God knows exactly what He's doing, we, not so much.

So yeah, I wish I had a different life. But at least God blessed me with others I'm proud to say are in my life. I then wish they were my parents, that's the part when I get depressed, basically because I want what I don't have, which sounds really selfish. Though I don't think it's too selfish to think the way I do. I love my dad. I just wish he was more like 'this or that guy', man I wish he was more like that guy, but, I have what I have, and I'm thankful for what I have.

Sometimes I wonder what God was thinking when he created the earth, like 'hey let's throw these people here and see what happens', why didn't we just go to heaven? I like to believe God wanted to have some fun on earth first. Like I bet he gets a kick out of watching people fall down the stairs. Not like he doesn't know it's gonna happen. He knows what I'm gonna be when I'm thirty, like, uh, can you tell me? I bet it's fun for Him, watching us and helping us make decisions, and hearing that we love Him. The best part is He always loves us even when we screw up. So maybe he wanted us to feel His love if we felt no other love, and wanted to give us choices, and new experiences.

****

My anxiety sucks; it's actually made me sick before. I went on a trip one time and had to stay in bed for two days because my anxiety was so bad it was making me physically sick. I felt like such a baby, I should've just worked it out. I felt so depressed and suicidal after that, but I talked it out with this guy, and he made me feel better. People told me to just calm down, I would try, but it's easier said than done.

Whenever my dad yells, I get anxiety and can't sleep or eat. Especially when I wake up to doors slamming or yelling, I jump awake after I could finally get some sleep, then I can't go back to sleep after that. Once you here and see your dad hitting your mom, you're never the same after that.

I wonder what he's gonna do next, what he's going to say, it's almost always the same.

"I hate my life, you F** B** I never wanna see you again, get a divorce, you don't make me happy, I'm gonna find another woman, call the cops!"

I don't know why I listen, if his voice makes me sick. I guess to hear if he hits my mom or not. Then I'll run out of my room and yell at him, which doesn't do much. He just yells at me then and threatens to hit me, sometimes I wish he would, go ahead, and see what happens.

I really hate when my dad is all mad one day, screaming at us, and the next day he could be totally fine. He always expects us to just forget what happened and act like nothing ever even happened. By this point, I just care that he's not yelling, though I'm still depressed when he's happy just not as bad, because how can you be boiling mad one day and fine the next? I think he's bipolar. I guess sleeping really does solve problems; I really need to figure out a solution to this depression problem, rather than drinking coffee all the time.

Well, sadly there isn't really an absolute cure to get rid of depression. You either need to take medication, therapy, or find things that make you happy. I guess then there is a cure to depression. What I'm saying is, it will always be apart of your life. If you were depressed at fifteen and are fine now at thirty, you will look back on yourself at fifteen and feel that depression again.

Life is not perfect. I believe everyone gets depressed at some point in their lives, it's now just a matter of how you handle it; will you show others you're depressed, or will you hide it? Will you get professional help, or try to help yourself?

I have actually googled some ways that help with depression I can say for myself, really worked, like working out. It keeps your mind off depression, focuses your brain muscles not on depression, and focuses on getting a healthy body. Caffeine is a chemical that is known to make you happy, preferably coffee, according to the article I read. Talking to people around you, they might have some good advice in helping you cope with depression. Getting out with friends, that's why we call them our friends, we like them and they make us feel better, and don't say they wanna kill us, or punch us.

The whole point in curing depression is to get your mind off depression, by finding things you like to do. If you're depressed because you don't like your family life, talk to someone about it, crash with friends or other family members, put yourself up for adoption. There is nothing that can "magically" make your home life better. If your parents argue or hit each other, they're most likely not going to listen to some kid to tell them to stop. But who am I to say they won't listen, won't know unless you try, try calling the cops, they get things done.

It's just crucial to read the situation, if your dad is the violent one; I wouldn't go up to him and tell him to stop hitting mommy. I would go to the calmer one, my mom, which I have, and all she says is, 'yeah I know, he's an idiot'; well okay then, I've tried. If they're both really violent, I would go tell a reliable person like a pastor or teacher. They should know what to do in situations like that, even tell someone if one person is really violent and the other does nothing to stop it...but that's just my opinion.

The reason we won't leave is because we feel trapped. I say we because I don't want to leave my mom alone with him because I don't trust him, therefore I feel trapped, as well.

My mom even said I should've left twenty years ago, but now I'm trapped.

I get that, other people may not get it, but I do. When most people see violence in a spouse, they leave their ass right away. But other people, like us, feel a sort of empathy for the douche bags. We stay with them saying things like 'it's not that bad' or 'it's how he/she shows emotion'. My favorite is, 'he's not like that all the time'. Yeah, well, twice is too many times, coming from someone who forgave her dad ten thousand freaking times; we just have too big of hearts I guess.

These men, or women, act nice after being a douche, just to stop us from leaving, I hate that. I want to be mad at you, but I can't because you're being nice, damn it! Sometimes I feel like saying to my mom, 'Either you leave him or I leave', don't know where I'll go but I'm leaving.

Leaving him would be kind of hard though, I would feel bad for him because then he would have no one. He puts it on himself though, yelling at everyone and chasing them away. My mom would also have to find another job, which she says nobody wants her because she's old, and she probably stops looking when my dad starts acting nice and pulls her in again. I don't know about the house, who would get it, or would we have to sell it, I don't know how this stuff works? I will miss this house though, plus we put so much work into it, getting new fencing and landscaping done, it looks really nice. Sometimes I feel bad leaving, other times I don't.

I can kind of sympathize for him I guess because he has diabetes, and you get crappy from diabetes, especially when your blood sugar is really high or low. I can't really tell him to get over it, because I don't have diabetes. But you can't get rid of it so learn to deal with it, yeah it might suck but it's not like it's a death sentence.

He does have other problems though, like drinking, and I think a doctor would tell him he's bipolar if he ever went to one.

"Doctors know shit! They just want you to pay them money."

Okay dad. They went to college for medicine so I'm pretty sure they know more than you. Meanwhile I wanna go to the doctor for everything.

"Mom I can barely walk on my foot I think I fractured it."

"You're fine, put some ice on it."

I keep bringing it up to them, until my dad yells, and then I stop and bear it out.

10

SATISFIED?

I was actually really excited coming to college, when I finally chose my college, I was so happy, and started imagining good things.

'I will find a boyfriend, I'll go to parties, I'll have the best roommates, I'll play in softball, I'll do well in school, and everyone will love me.'

Well, that only came true for my roommates. Yes, I didn't really like them at first. But as I got to know them, they were pretty cool. But of course my one roommate who I hung out with a lot took a semester off, so now I have one roommate, not two. The reason I missed my one roommate so much, is because we found things to laugh about, complained about people, complain about guys, not going to parties, are both lazy, and procrastinated a lot.

'Can those people shut up out there? Hey remember that Vine with those two drunk guys? People are so stupid. Why can't we find parties? I was gonna go to this thing but now I don't wanna go. You wanna go play pool?'

It wasn't the same when she left, I just found more things to talk about with her, and our conversations would always lead to other conversations that would keep us laughing and talking for hours. I remember one time we were at this speech we had to go to for English, about the guy who wrote the book we had to read over the summer. We stayed for about thirty minutes. I asked her if she wanted to leave, she said yeah. Got up, walked down the first step, and fell down the rest, we were in the back so nobody saw except us and some other professors, which I think made it funnier. We both couldn't stop laughing, and we had to be quite so we were laughing but making no sound, we laughed for about ten minutes, and all the way back to our dorm.

Now I got nothing to do but homework and softball, and a little free time to hang out with my one other friend that's still here. Things were so much better when she was around, just because we would talk while studying, or instead of studying. She was the complete opposite of me. She was loud and didn't care what others thought of her. I was quiet and cared what people thought of me. But being with her, I acted more like her. I became a little louder, and not caring what people thought of me, now I hang out with my one other friend and she's the best, and makes life so much better.

I need to start not caring what people think of me, I won't be complete until that happens. I hear people talk about others so much, 'this girl said this, this girl doesn't like this'. There's so much pressure to say the right thing, and I don't wanna offend anyone, so I just say nothing.

I would invite myself to a party, but what if the person says yes just because they don't wanna be rude and say no? That's the main reason I won't invite myself to a party. Plus, I already think of them as bitches because they won't invite me, and I've been dropping hints I want to go to parties, but they obviously don't pick them up.

This one volunteering thing we had to do for softball, I overheard this girl talking about a party, so I told her to text me if she's going or not. Later that night she texted me that she's not going, alright cool, at least she texted me. I was getting ready for bed, scrolling through Snapchat, and I saw her at what looked like a party. I was so mad, I told my roommate, and we were both pissed at her, I guess that was her hint that she didn't want me there, so I gave up. That little bitch, everyone thinks she's soooo cute because she's 4'10, nobody ever thinks I'm cute and it kind of hurts, nobody like me. I'm probably weird and look scary. I'm also insecure about my face.

My head is way too big. My face looks crooked. Maybe I'll feel better when I feel more secure about my appearance, I feel great most of the time now, so that's good, it's just all in my big head I have.

I guess nobody wants me, I tried. My mom says I don't try to make friends. Invite yourself to a party she says. I tried but it didn't work, 'try again', I don't want to bug them, but I guess that's what I'll have to do to go to a party. Maybe if I invite myself they'll realize how awesome I really am?

I'm so pissed everyone is out having fun except me. I just sit in my room on weekends watching TV. I order in a pizza sometimes, my roommates go home for the weekend, which is nice because I have the place to myself. My mom texts me, and reminds me of how boring I am.

"You need to go make some friends, be more outgoing, invite yourself to a party, you're a really fun person, I hate when your alone, you're always alone."

Thanks mom for reminding me I have no friends. This is why I thought about transferring to another school, one with a sorority, so it'll be easier to make friends and go to parties. The reason I want to go to parties so much, is because I become more talkative and outgoing once I get a few drinks in me. I guess I'm being good, not going to parties, being a good child of God while everyone else is drinking and having sex, anyone ever think I wanna do that? No way, who would think of me? I guess I'm just as bad thinking about partying. I drink alone in my room sometimes, smoking, meeting guys on Tinder (which I was so desperate to get and regret it), and getting drunk with my mom and relatives when they come to visit. I look forward to them coming up; it's nice and fun to see them coming to see me at college. We'd have fun and go to bars and shopping together, I love when they come up, I party with them instead, and it's probably more fun that way.

I already got taken advantage in college so I guess that's one thing, the bastard stole a hundred from my wallet, he used me for what he wanted, stole my money and left. I haven't been on Tinder since. Not even that guy liked me, so why would anyone else? I'm done, if people want me they will come to me, if not, screw them.

My mom loves reminding me I'm alone every weekend and it makes her sad. First of all, the parties are in driving distance and I have no car, and I have no friends who go to parties. Plus, I do talk to people, just not as much as others, as much as a shy person talks. I just don't invite myself along with people when they do stuff, like we didn't invite you. What if I ask them to tag along, but they don't want me to ask to tag along? People tend to say 'yeah it's fine if you do this' when it's really not. They might say it's cool if I go with them, but they really don't want me to come, and that's my fear. I need to learn to face my fear; I like being alone sometimes anyway.

It does bug me a little hearing; people talking about parties and drinking in front of me.

"That party was so fun!"

"I drank too much last night."

"This guy was so wasted."

"I forgot to take my birth control because you can't take it when you drink."

We get it. You drink and have sex. And I can't forget the Snapchat stories, everyone out having fun while I'm just in bed looking at memes. I don't wanna go to those parties anyway, a bunch of bitches and stupid guys, I'll just party with my family, I like them more anyway. You know it's bad when your mom wants you to go to parties. Since when was college all about that? If I hear one more party story about a party, I'm going to explode.

I get so upset hearing about parties sometimes. I just can't take it. I wish I was like other people, outgoing, pretty, and fun. I guess I'm not that fun to others, I think I'm fun, once you get to know me, I may look all serious but trust me, I'm really not.

Anyway, college should be about learning and getting an education. I'm doing badly in my classes and I'm not even going to parties, I'm just stupid and lazy.

People can go to parties, do good in school, and are great at sports, and what am I? Pretty damn good at being lazy that's what. I honestly don't know if I'll ever be okay with my life, I already screwed up so many times and missed chances. Though I try not to think about those things, 'the past is in the past', as everybody always says. Sometimes I think about that too much though, like when my coach asks us what happened in the game last night, I don't know that was the past, and God says to forget the past. I need to live for today. Maybe that's why sports aren't my thing. Coaches need to understand, I may not be that great in practice, but I'm much different in a game. If you would just play me, and who cares what we did last game, that was the past, maybe we'll start winning then? I do well in practices, I hit the ball good and get on base, but does he play me? No. Screw this I'm taking up band.

****

Softball is over now, and now I don't know what to do with my life, I mean I didn't really know before, but still. While doing softball, I felt like I was actually doing something productive with my life, even if softball wasn't the best, now I feel so unproductive. I like the free time, but it seems too much. Especially on Mondays, Wednesdays and Fridays when I get off at 11:30; I usually nap, watch TV, play games on my phone, watch YouTube, or walk to places with my friend, if it's bearable out.

I guess my moms right, softball gives me something to do and helped me get my mind off things, but so will band, at least I hope. I kind of hate that she's right, like I feel like she'd always planned I'd do softball in college, ever since I was a freshman in high school. Shit, I could've got a band scholarship for this school since I had no chance for softball, considering my coach never played me in high school.

I honestly don't know how next year will go. I'll probably end up dropping classes again, and getting the same GPA in high school, sometimes I don't know how they let me go to this school.

I honestly don't care at this point, I'm here, and need to make the best of it, which I'm beginning to. I'm much better now from the first few weeks of school, when I cried every night, wanted to go home, very depressed and confused, I don't cry as much now…let's see what next year brings.

I'm probably in a better mood because there's only like a week left now, and I'm counting the hours till I can go home, it's currently 120 hours.

I guess this year could've gone a lot worse. It went fast but slow, like by second semester I felt like I should've been a sophomore, yet I can't really believe I'm already done now and a sophomore in college practically. I didn't really know what I was doing here the first couple of weeks. I just thought college is a must and is how people get good jobs, ounce I get those thoughts in my mind and trust God; I know I'm in the right place.

****

I could say I honestly don't know how things could change for the better. I got through my freshman year of college. I guess that's the only thing I have going for me. Most people would say there's a lot more that I have, but I don't have what I want, nothing seems to make me happy, and I want a new family. I feel selfish saying that, because I have my best friend at college who cheers me up, my health and generous parents (even though they bug me sometimes). I get in these moods a lot when my parents are in a bad mood, I just want everyone to be happy but that doesn't seem to be the case.

My mom came in my room the other day and said she was upset but didn't know why, so I started guessing why she was upset.

"Is it because of me?

"No"

"Is it because you're bored?"

"No."

"Is it because of dad and you wish you had a different husband?"

"Yeah, kind of…"

Me too, well a new dad in my case. Whether that's true or not, I honestly don't know. Because he could be yelling and screaming tonight, and be completely fine the next day and act like nothing ever happened, or he would joke about what happened.

"Why was I mad at you again? Oh well I don't know why I get like that, I guess I'm just depressed and feel like I have no one, ha-ha-ha-ha."

So he makes us feel bad, and we're 'back to normal' again. I really hate when he does that. He doesn't apologize, he just expects us to forgive him, or he just thinks if he acts normal we will too, because now we just care about making him happy.

The reason she won't leave him is because he acts nice to her sometimes and drags her back in. And they've been together for like thirty-years, and why throw that away just over some domestic violence?

I've talked to enough people, and they all pretty much say to just deal with it or move out. I've tried two times to fix this, and only the one time really worked, so I'm about done now. I've somehow dealt with this shit since I was two years old, not telling anybody, and being somewhat happy; can really screw a person up. I guess now I'm just waiting for the world to end and eternal peace to happen. For the meantime, I'm trying to enjoy my life down here. It just sucks though when I want a life so badly that I don't have. Then I make myself depressed. People always say 'oh just don't think that way your life isn't that bad', the ones who usually say that aren't in my position, and it's easier said than done, but good advice.

I'm an adult now according to the state, and need to make my own life happen. I think I'm doing a decent job at it, trying to get a career, to make money to pay to live; it's what you make of it. Life's too short to worry about things, so I'm learning to not worry and leave things in God's hands. Yeah my life's not perfect, but whose is? At least I tried to fix my life, and made a little improvement. It sucks that my dad yells and my family isn't happy all the time. But we are most of the time when my dads not yelling and it's great when we are happy. I just go along for the ride now, trust God, and do things that make me happy, because he has a plan, and makes no mistakes. Everything happens for a reason.

I may not be where I want to be now, but I will soon be.

11

PART TWO

So the guy was right, sophomore year was a little better, I guess things do get better with time. I kind of hate it when other people are right, because most of the time it means I'm wrong. I obviously didn't transfer, and am rooming now with my one friend I met at college, who didn't move away. I think I found out what I want to major in…and things are foggy about softball. I did give it another shot, working out and practicing with the team, but after a week or so of no sleep, I decided to quit…my mom wouldn't talk to me for three days.

Softball is different now, and I'm tired and actually want to get some sleep…and practicing this whole time just to not play in the games seems pointless to me. Yes, I'm still just as negative, thinking I won't get better, and that the coach will never play me.

But yeah, at least I made kind of an adult decision…plus my head isn't pounding as much anymore. I also figured out I like helping people, so that's what I'll major in Human Social Services, which is kind of like psychology, but with less academia. How can you not be good at helping people? I helped a lot of people…everybody helps someone at least, even if it's just talking nonsense with them, and just being there for company. Plus we learn about messed up families and people, so I have experience with that…

Well yeah, I guess I was bad at helping people, because I didn't end up majoring in Human Social Services. I'm still over-thinking in my classes as much as I did freshman year. Just now I'm thinking more of what I want to do for the rest of my life, rather than thinking about death…

‘Wow, doctors in the 1800’s really stuck a needle in your brain to try and cure you from mental illness? Well at least they don’t do that anymore. Bad kids used to get sent to prison for a day to try to get them to behave better…Why don’t we do that anymore?’

We watched a whole season of the reality series ‘Scared Straight’. It was exactly what it sounds like. Kids being scared into acting straight… not mistaken as being straight rather than being gay, but straight as in acting well-behaved… Okay, maybe I explained it a little wrong. I was intrigued every second while watching it, imagining me in that chair, being screamed at by the prison lady, who had dreadlocks and tattoos all over her.

The show actually worked, the kids who were sent there behaved after being screamed at for an hour; I guess scaring people does change them (hopefully for the better.) I was maybe relating a little, because people yelling at me did make me change. Like this one time on the way to school. I was in a mood, and was complaining about people having these nicer things than me. Then my mom who was driving me, screamed at me to stop complaining and be grateful. So you can say she scared me straight I guess.

The show was so good; I went back to my dorm after class and watched the other episodes on YouTube.

****

I do need to stop complaining though…and thinking. I probably went back to the guy in about a month after I started school.

“You just need to not think.”

Okay, I’ll stop thinking, and most likely fail everything (rather than just one class.) I guess what he meant was don’t over-think…yeah, I’ll try I guess, but then I’ll think about not thinking, and think why I over think, then think about how not thinking is making me act.

I'm doing it again…I'm thinking about why I even talk with this guy? I feel like we've been through a lot and I've told him a lot, except I think of him as a father figure. What else I learned in my Human Social Service class was transferring, which is having feelings for your therapist (which I'm probably doing.) I really can't help it, I get too attached to people, and maybe I'll change someday…It's not that bad.

12

THE OTHER YEAR

Sophomore year is the year; the year where another person dies, the year with the pandemic, the year where I'll pick the right major, the year where I became happier. My dad threw me into a wall the night before I left for my second year…But at least I'm friends with my so-called friend again. It was probably three months in, when I was crying in my bed, until I got a text from her saying hi. We started talking, and then eventually we moved onto apologizing for punching each other. I knew we'd make up, I'm happier now…I think? Is it weird to not know if you're happy or not…What even are feelings? Well, if I don't think, does that mean I don't think about my feelings? Oh, God, help me…that's it; I'll just think about God for now, and pray for relief of my mind.

I've been going to chapel more this year. I remember my freshman year when I asked my roommate if we could go to chapel together…she said yeah, but left without me, so I cried on my bed instead. I actually went by myself one time, which I'm still surprised about today, and the little sermon was perfect. It was about life and how it's hard, but go to God, and everything will eventually be okay. It really spoke to me, especially being the timid freshman that I was; I left feeling maybe about 30% better…which is something.

I'm glad I actually have someone to go to chapel with me this year, someone who will actually wait for me. What I know about being a Christian is you should go to church/chapel to stay steadfast in your faith, and I could honestly say I feel much better after church. I like being reminded why I'm alive, and how much I'm loved.

I don't know why, but this year is better than last year. Maybe I just needed to get the one 'big change' year out of the way? Plus I found some people to help me through things- also I found that therapy place that had weird directions to; I guess talking really does help.

So I found ways to cope through this shit, and found out I should be proud of surviving these things. So I'm cured. Well, I don't follow directions very well, so maybe I'm not so cured. Can I really be 'cured'? No, probably not. So I'm back to crying and complaining, which what good does that do…Again, at least I got people to talk and complain to. Sometimes I think I just find things to complain about? Maybe because if I complain, people will give me advice, but like my friend said, no one will talk to me if I complain all the time.

I'll just bring up other people, try to learn about them. I need to learn to talk to people, and complaining all the time to people isn't the best way to meet new people - I should get to know them before I complain. Do most people in college have to learn to talk to people? I ended up majoring in talking to people.

Okay, I got through freshman year. Stressing about all these jobs I could potentially get. Talking to all these college professors and therapists, only to find out I don't have to decide this right now. I should only focus on the basics, like learning the thousands of people in history, taking a gym class which will never be related to my future job, and taking theology classes. Okay, so I'll get my gen-ed classes out of the way, then everything will just come into play, right? I guess I'll find out in time.

I literally should not be here, I feel like I'm too confused of a person to be here in college. Everybody is confused when they're in college…but I feel like I'm really confused. I'm still thinking about these 101 different jobs I could get. I'm thinking about my family life. I'm thinking about how I should stop complaining. I'm thinking about softball still. I'm thinking about band, thinking about if I should study or not, thinking about what I should wear for the next three days and what I should eat, I literally think about everything.

Whatever, it's fine; I'll just go to this other funeral to calm my head.

13

THINKING

It was probably in the evening when everyone got this email saying he passed away, another person on softball. I wasn't weirdly jealous this time at least, but I was thinking about other people and their relationship with him, and how I shouldn't be there. I mean, he was the coach, everybody knew him. I wonder what they're thinking of majoring in. Enough, I need to focus on this funeral…or not focus, just feel emotion. Usually when I think too much like this, I just end up spacing out, just sitting there blankly, crying and covering my face with my hair.

I think the most in my sleep. If I have a dream that I have this test coming up, I'll panic all night long. I'll think about softball still, think about the classes I'm in and why I have to take math, think about life and the regrets I have for calling the cops on my dad. I'll think about everything at night, and then I'll be fine the next morning (I sound like I'm my dad.) I've wasted a good night's rest from thinking again…sometimes I forget I'm not supposed to think.

Every time someone dies I think way too much, especially because people say death comes in three, which I don't really believe, because it's a hoax everyone and their grandma believe. It's like when my mom says that my dad will get angry because it's a full moon-he does-but I think everyone just gets psyched out… this is why I hate these hoaxed theories. The weird family I went out vacation with had this thing called 'Murphy's Law' which is some weird thing that if you go this way, this hazard will happen.

"We got stuck by all this traffic because of Murphy's Law"

Literally the only way I know about 'the law' is because of them, not from my fancy college classes. I really refuse to believe all that voodoo shit. Yeah, your brain messes with you, but saying and knowing all these voodoo tactics like Murphy's Law will just mess with you more-especially me who thinks a lot.

So maybe it does happen in three? No, we just psych ourselves out and believe what thousands of other people and fancy psychologists are saying. Maybe that's my problem, I don't believe? Oh gosh, I don't know, stop thinking.

I need to think, I'm in college. I need to think about my future and forget the past… and stop crying. Maybe me thinking so much is why I can't decide on a major? I always pick things at the last minute, or think about what I should have done after it already happened…I decided on a major basically my senior year, and it wasn't the best decision.

This whole college thing is starting to bug me a little; I'm really just here because it's the 'thing to do.' Growing up, it was 100% that I was going to college somewhere. 'This is the first milestone to being on your own', 'you have to get a good job to make a good living', 'are you happy?' Shouldn't you have some idea of what you want to do before you go to college? I thought I did, but everyone made fun of my potential majors (not counting the fact I was bad at chemistry).

'What are you going to do with an Environmental science degree, hug a tree?' What are you going to do as a dietitian; no one even goes to those?'

Okay, no one goes to a dietitian, fine I won't major in that then. What's the point of life anymore? You work and work, and for what, money to spend again? I'm over everything right now and who needs who. I have to think of so many things and get things straight. No one needs a dietitian? Okay, cross that off. Environmental Science is stupid and I'll make no money? Okay, cry, and cross that off. I'm bad at this, cross that off, bad at that, cross that off. Can I cross myself off yet? No. There are reasons I won't do that. The list of things I can't do is longer than the list of things I can do at this point. I'll just take a walk with my roommate, and stress about not doing homework that I should be doing.

***

I really need to find things I'm good at…other than complaining. I'm good at the trumpet, and kind of good at helping people (just not good enough to major in). So I have a second semester to look forward to. I'm joining band, moving into the sophomore year apartment with my roommate, and things will be a little better.

14

THE BIG ONE

I moved into the apartment and got my own stove, big living room, own bathroom, and more space that I have to share with three other people. I like my original roommate, but the other girls are just alright. I'm pretty sure they don't like me…I just get that vibe. Remember to stop thinking.

I still haven't given the idea up on writing a book…until I found how much it costs to actually publish one, plus the thought of it not being good enough. Great, that unrealistic dream is crushed. I just want to be really into something and motivated to do something. There is literally nothing I'm motivated to do; besides go to my meetings where I can complain.

I'm motivated to play the trumpet and listen to music. I'm only a third trumpet, but I like it and I feel a part of something. I still feel awkward of course though, because the band director signals sections out sometimes to play, and if I do something wrong, I'll get down, then cry about it later. There are also about thirty people in the band, and I get anxious if there are more than three people in a room…but I just have to remember to not think, which does help actually. I don't think about others, and walk in like I belong there. I can't believe people get paid to talk to others? That was a random thing to say pertaining to what I was talking about, but that's me. I own my randomness.

This year went back to the 1900's. It was right before spring break when I heard our classmate, who went to China, probably wasn't coming back for a while. Because there's this virus outbreak that happened, and they won't let people leave the country. Well about a week or so during spring break, we were told not to come back because of the Chinese virus spreading to America (I guess they let people leave the country.) Wow, I moved into my new apartment, and they kick us out…Murphy's Law. Now I get to go back home, yay!

I guess it was good I went home, because my mom got sick, and I had to work with my dad, double yay! I was super sad to hear about my mom, but even sadder that I had to work with that man…which I guess wasn't horrible…Just listening to complaints about doctors got pretty old. Those doctors are taking care of your wife who you love so much, so I would really stop talking. This is why I question everything.

"Doctors really don't know anything, the nurses know more, we pay them all this money and they don't know anything, but they're making mama better, which is a good thing."

I really don't understand this man, and think he's bipolar. So if no one really knows anything why are we wasting our money and believing their lies? How do we even know what's good for us anyway when there are 101 different psychologists telling us different things to do? Pick up a crying baby, let them cry it out, eat three meals a day. It's better to just eat snacks throughout the day, having a shot a day makes you live longer… which there is evidence of, she lived to 103.

This year I was sad 24/7, because I had to work with my dad and my mom was in the hospital. My dad would call her every day to ask her what she does, so he can work two jobs-or learn the other part of his job that he doesn't do. Yeah, you say she doesn't do anything, yet you call her to ask her how to send an email? Just what a sick person needs, yelling. Whatever…God, just make her better.

I'm honestly a little mad at Him right now for all this, but just need to know He did this all for a reason, and I know that now. He knows I'm mad, but I know He still loves me, and I'll get over this.

I'm probably more than half my dad, when I get mad I feel like him… maybe that's why I'm so mad at Him? One time I was upset, and my mom said I'm just like my dad… then I went to my room and cried. I just don't want to be like him and have this horrible anxiety that leads to anger…and I don't want diabetes.

So I gotta do classes from home now, should be better right? Not really. I still fail open note tests. My mom even did a test for me, proving that psychology was 'so easy, well guess what, she failed too…thanks. This is actually worse than in person classes. I need physical interaction. All this shit had to happen in April, where it was raining half the month. So now I can't even go outside…seriously, God, what is going on? No one actually knows what's going on exactly, and per usual, there are so many opinions flying around.

'Wear a mask, don't wear a mask. Wash your hands 24/7, it's fine, we need to build our immune systems. The president is a nut, no; he's the smartest one we ever had.'

I've always been a confused person, but I think there comes a point to confusion, where you just say screw it, that's fine, then go with the flow and choose whatever. This is so much right now… is the World ending? Well now it's probably not gonna end because I said it…or maybe it will end because I said it? Thinking God will know that, so He won't end it…but maybe He will end it anyway, because he thinks that I think it won't end now? I'm done with everything, even God I think. No, wait, I can't do that, He's the only person who believes in me and loves me 1000%.

So people are stuck at home being lazy, because they don't really have another option…'But how do they still make money'? Well, I guess the government does have money to give away rather than take it, and ended up giving us stimulus checks.

****

So, I'm stuck at home with my dad for a while, not really ever thinking I would. It is kind of very awkward, the house just isn't the same…trying to do my homework online (which is also what I never really thought I would do.) At least I got my family sending us food and positive thoughts, reminding me how God will lead us through this. My dad I guess could have been worse during this whole fiasco; he could have actually killed somebody, rather than just threatening. Being the angry person that he is, I knew when she had cancer, that he would get mad, I just didn't know how mad.

He still would put her down every now and then, like she's not already down. He would still expect her to cook three meals a day…and yeah, the way she gets thanked for it is a little weird…being called a lazy b. How they made it this far, I really don't know; I guess its 'true love ' (or they just can't find anyone else).

I was so appalled by his behavior; I went to live with my grandma for like a month, over-thinking every day: should I be here? Am I being over dramatic? It's not all his fault; it's just the way he is. I need to be home with my mom.

At least school was over, and I squeaked by in psychology by some miracle, and we can go back to in person school next year, if the virus didn't kill everyone by then. At least my mom has the non-deadliest kind of cancer. At least I have a roof over my head. At least I have a start on my resume. It's good to think of the positive…At least I got to spend time with my grandma, talking about her son and his problems…which was a little awkward. Complaining to her about her son was like telling her the latest gossip, but trying not to offend her because it involves her friend. She understands it the most though at least, and knows his problems, so it was pretty nice talking about all this.

I guess it's the same with my mom and dad, they know each other the most, and so that's probably why they'll never leave. They know what makes each other mad, but will say them anyway.

Maybe that's the thing to do? Just getting things off your chest, and making the other person mad; secrets to a long lasting relationship (I think).

I moved back home before school started in August. At least my grandma lived a block away. So when I was living there, I could still see my mom and we could get coffee together, then said farewell while she went back to him. At least she made it clear she wasn't choosing him over me, he just needed her more than me, which whatever it's cool.

So yay, we get to go back to school…and wear masks, so we don't get sick, even though we did, because a piece of cloth over your mouth can help so much. I had to play the trumpet with a mask on, which how do you do that? I figured it out. I was 100 times happier just being around actual people, and sleeping in my dorm bed, which for some reason I loved so much.

At least my mom was only sick for about 4 months (even though it seemed longer), but that's just because things dragged because of "the virus." I knew we would eventually get over all this.

15

AT LAST

So, I'm back at school and everything is great…the end.

I HAVE to pick a major and stick to it…so I chose the easiest major, which is basically talking, and I'm barely good at that. This is when I look at the big picture. How at the end nothing will matter but Jesus. Though that may be true, I still need to pick a major that will get me a good job, and cause me to not live with my parents forever. Honestly, I am thinking more of marrying rich at this point, but you can't really plan that…bummer. It worked for this one girl at my conservative college…man I should've taken Spanish, and then maybe I would've ended up marrying the Spanish professor.

When I heard this, I was very obsessed and jealous…and mostly confused how this was allowed. If this was a public school they both would have probably been kicked out, but not in this Jesus loving college.

At last, I finally picked a major, very late into my college year. I guess you can say I settled. I minored in communication, and then switched to majoring in it, because I couldn't-or was too unmotivated-to major in Human Social Services. Everyone obviously downed that major, and had their theories on how I wouldn't find a good job… they made me cry a lot, one time I was at a restaurant, which was pretty embarrassing. Whatever, if I change now, I'll have to take another year, and it's the motivation thing that won't allow me to do that.

It'll all be fine, I'll find a job, eventually, and God is with me, I have my loving parents to go back to. I have my friends to rant to, track literally made me cry, in my meeting with the communication department, even they seemed like they didn't have confidence in me.

"So what do you plan on doing with your communication degree?"

"Well, I'm not sure if I have an exact plan, but I know I will have a steadier plan after learning more information in my classes."

"This major is very broad, and I'm just curious why you picked this major when you don't really talk in class?"

Ouch! That's what got me. Yeah, it probably didn't seem like the biggest hurtful thing to say, but for me it did. I was questioning everything; tearing up…thank God I had a mask on to cover half my face. They obviously knew I was emotional, because I was sinking back in my chair, and they made it a point to say they 'weren't trying to discourage me' (which made me feel more discouraged). I honestly don't know why I decided to major in this. It is so easy to offend me, it irritates me.

I just know things will work out in the end; I need to stop thinking and enjoy life, maybe focus on my faith a little more. At least I and my friend are both still deciding on things, so we have things in common, and I'm not the only one confused about things. We give each other advice, and both feel better about things at the end (or just both agree we'll struggle together). One of the main things she says to me is not to worry, and how things will come together in the end. Which I am 100% sure of (changes may vary).

EPILOGUE

These years have been 100% crazy and 100% not what I expected, but that's what makes life interesting right? I'm just going with the flow of things at this point, no more 'this is my year, a new year, a new, me', I can't just magically be a new person each year? That sounds like too much work anyway, being a new person every year.

When I first started college, I had all these high hopes of things, got all these matching pink pens, notebooks, blankets, had hopes of going to parties, living confidently on my own. Things obviously didn't go as planned, when I said good-bye to my mom, I cried for an hour, and every day after that, and I never went to any parties.

Everything's thankfully worked out with time, and my dramatic episodes faded. I still think too much, and will probably never get over that, but I know things will keep getting better, because they have before. You have to rust someone for things falling into place, and I trust God, even if it was my mom who helped me pass the class by emailing the professor to give me the .2 grade to help me pass psychology, it was also God… who gave my professor the feeling of generosity to give me the 'free push' so that I would pass. COVID happened for a reason. My mom getting sick happened for a reason. They happened at the same time for a reason. COVID walked so that I could run, run home to help my mom and dad with their business. So I guess there's the upside to all this. It's really easy to find the negative in things, but only a few can find the upside to things (and yeah, I know I've complained a lot at this point).

I know that I am 100% thankful and grateful for every little thing in my life, positive and negative.

No more writing things in my journal in hoping to write a book. There'll be no more worrying about if I'll get a job once I graduate. No more trying so hard to fit in. No more yelling to try to change my entire life. No more worrying about other people, no more having anxiety when I'm with a group of people, no more 'this will be my year'. I am who I am, and that's who I am. Moving on! Chapter two!

THE END

Advantage
BOOKS

www.ingramcontent.com/pod-product-compliance
Lightning Source LLC
LaVergne TN
LVHW021525080426
835509LV00018B/2667

* 9 7 8 1 5 9 7 5 5 7 9 3 1 *